LESSONS IN DRAG

The **MANDEL LECTURES** *in the* **HUMANITIES**

at **BRANDEIS UNIVERSITY**

Sponsored by the Jack, Joseph and Morton Mandel Foundation

DIRECTOR, PROFESSOR ULKA ANJARIA

The Mandel Lectures in the Humanities were launched in the fall of 2011 to promote humanistic inquiry at Brandeis University, following the 2010 opening of the new Mandel Center for the Humanities. The lectures bring to the Mandel Center each year an influential scholar or scholar-practitioner who gives a series of lectures on topics of broad interest for a range of campus audiences. The Mandel Lectures are unique in their celebration of cutting-edge topics, forms, and modes of inquiry in the arts, humanities, and humanistic social sciences: the speakers have ranged from historians and literary critics to performance artists, writers, and anthropologists. The published series of books reflects the interdisciplinary mission of the Center and the wide range of extraordinary work being done in the humanities today.

For a complete list of books that are available in the series, visit https://brandeisuniversitypress.com/series/mandel-lectures.

Kareem Khubchandani, *Lessons in Drag*
Colm Tóibín, *On James Baldwin*
Dipesh Chakrabarty, *One Planet, Many Worlds: The Climate Parallax*
Nancy Langston, *Climate Ghosts: Migratory Species in the Anthropocene*
David Der-wei Wang, *Why Fiction Matters in Contemporary China*
Wendy Doniger, *The Donigers of Great Neck: A Mythologized Memoir*
Ingrid D. Rowland, *The Divine Spark of Syracuse*
James Wood, *The Nearest Thing to Life*
David Nirenberg, *Aesthetic Theology and Its Enemies: Judaism in Christian Painting, Poetry and Politics*

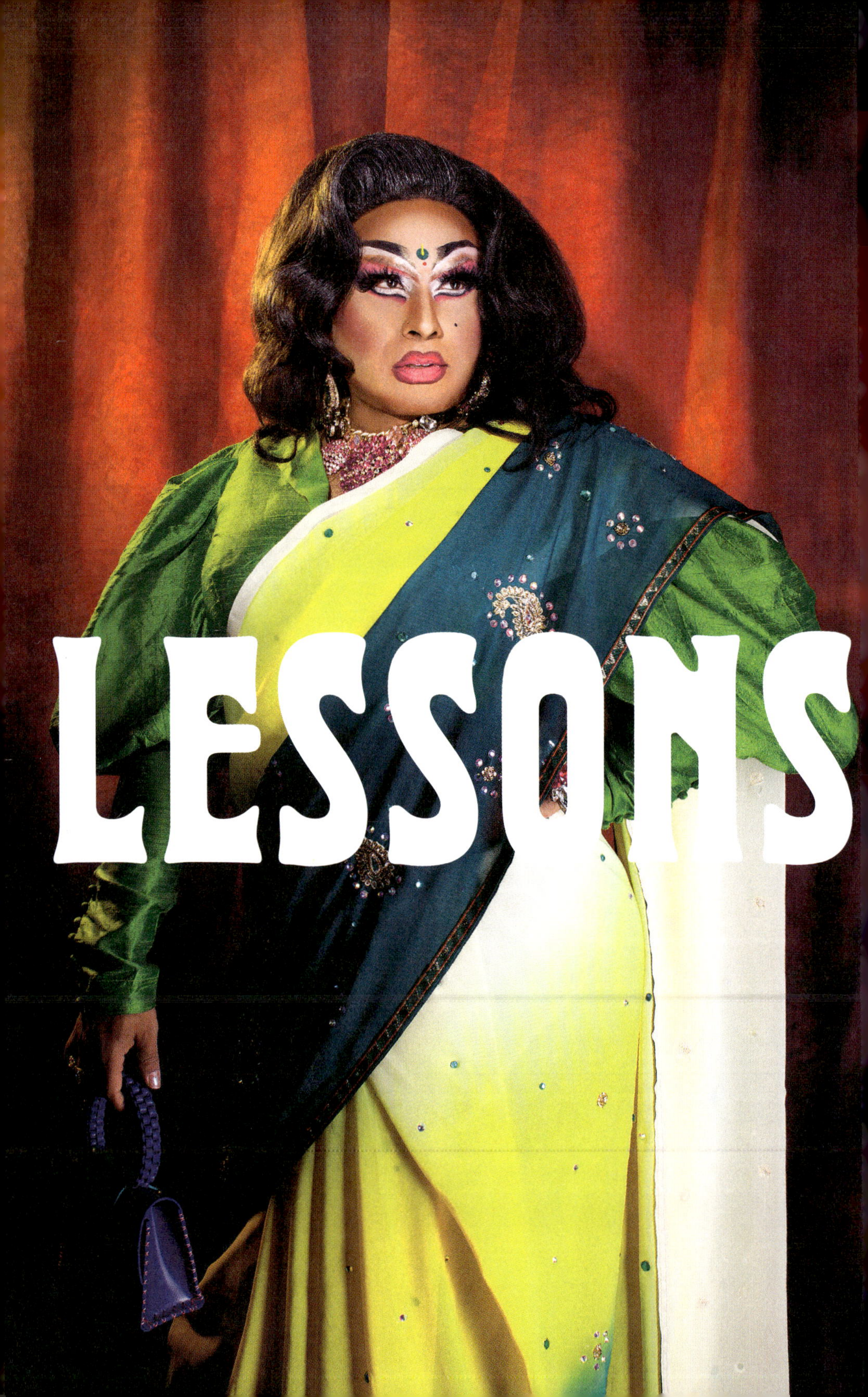
LESSONS

KAREEM KHUBCHANDANI

with LaWhore Vagistan

IN DRAG

A Queer Manual for Academics, Artists, and Aunties

Brandeis University Press / Waltham, MA

Brandeis University Press

Manufactured in the United States of America
Designed and composed in Arek Latin and Basic Gothic Pro
by Mindy Basinger Hill

Library of Congress Cataloging-in-Publication Data
Names: Khubchandani, Kareem, 1982- author | LaWhore Vagistan, 1982- author
Title: Lessons in drag : a queer manual for academics, artists, and aunties /
Kareem Khubchandani ; with LaWhore Vagistan.
Description: Waltham, MA : Brandeis University Press, [2025] | Series: The
Mandel Lectures in the Humanities at Brandeis University | Includes
bibliographical references. | Summary: "This book delves into the lessons drag
practice offers about academia-shaping approaches to research, teaching, and
writing-while revealing how scholarship influences drag
performances, and inspiring understanding of fashion, music, divas, and
aunties"—Provided by publisher.
Identifiers: LCCN 2025024281 (print) | LCCN 2025024282 (ebook) |
ISBN 9781684582891 paperback | ISBN 9781684582907 ebook
Subjects: LCSH: Drag performance—Study and teaching | Research—
Philosophy
Classification: LCC PN1969.D73 K48 2025 (print) | LCC PN1969.D73 (ebook)
LC record available at https://lccn.loc.gov/2025024281
LC ebook record available at https://lccn.loc.gov/2025024282

5 4 3 2 1

CONTENTS

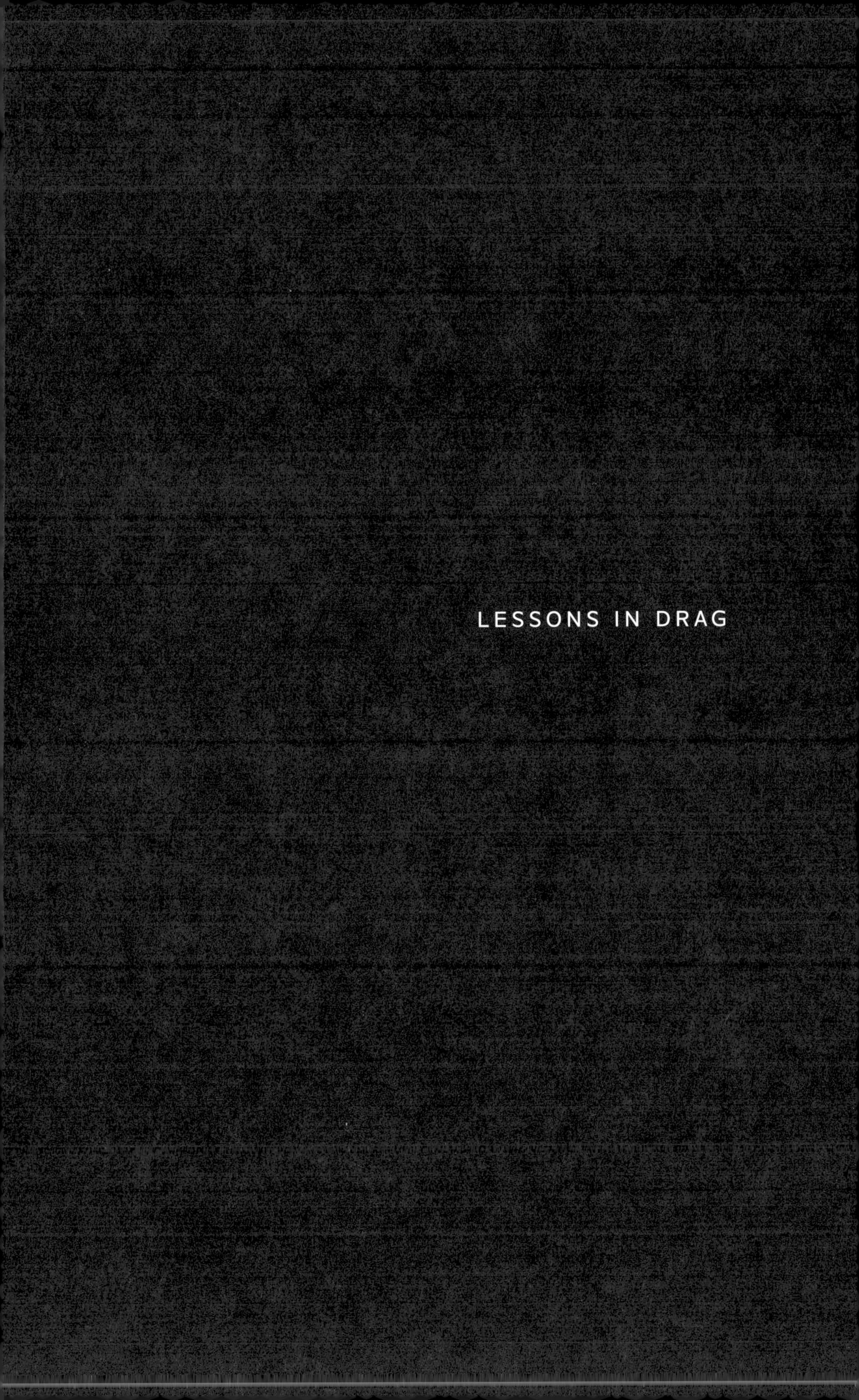

LESSONS IN DRAG

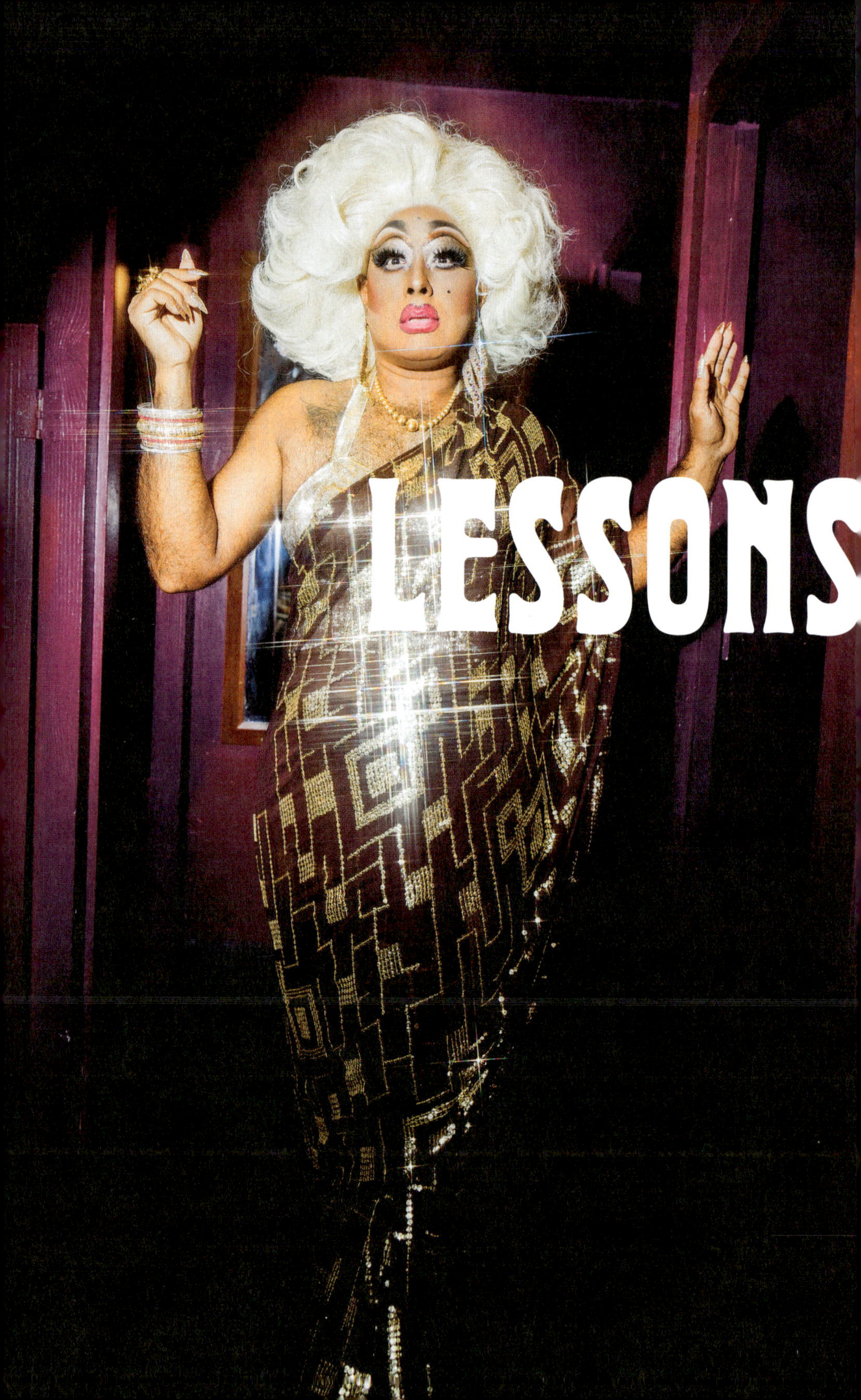

LESSONS

IN DRAG

THE INTERVIEW, THE SHOW, THE BOOK

LaWhore Vagistan So. Professor. We meet again?

Kareem Khubchandani Always a pleasure, Aunty.

LV You're looking well. You've put on weight?

KK LaWhore?!

LV It's OK. So have I. Being fat is not a bad thing . . .

KK Super aunty of you to make a comment about weight first thing.

LV And being an aunty . . .

KK Is not a bad thing. I know, I know, I wrote the boo . . .

LV You're *still* writing the book.

KK OMG, I'm leaving!

LV Sit!

KK [*sits*]

LV You're writing a *different* book? Not the "aunty" book?

KK [*nods sheepishly*]

LV Everyone is waiting for the aunty book.

KK Let them wait. I need to get this one out of my system . . .

LV Like a good shit.

KK LaWhore!

LV [*sips her tea*]

KK Listen, I wanted to ask if you'd also be a part of this book?

LV I already wrote for the *Decolonize* book. You want another "Introduction" from me? You can't ask your Sasha Velours and Aloks to write?

KK No, like will you write the book *with* me? Like, write chapters.

LV Hmmm. Will my name be on the cover?

KK I haven't yet talked to the edi . . .

LV Will my name be on the cover?

KK [*relents*] Yes.

LV Then yes.

KK OK, amazing. So, the book asks "What does drag teach us about X?" What does drag teach us about being an academic, or simply about being in the world? Drag, as a practice *and* a way of seeing the world, is incredibly instructive about how to navigate everything from the interpersonal to the institutional. I know I'm not telling *you* anything new. But ya, the broad frame is that drag is pedagogy, and pedagogy is drag. The book is going to be called *Lessons in Drag*.

LV Like my show!

KK Exactly. And also like our first conversation . . .

LV Interview.

KK Ya, interview, with you and me. That was *also* called "Lessons in Drag."

LV Remind me. It was such a long time ago.

KK It was 2015.

LV Exactly! I was in my wigless era. Very avant-garde, very edgy, very Joey Jay!

Drag, as a practice *and* a way of seeing the world, is incredibly instructive about how to navigate everything from the interpersonal to the institutional.

KK Right. So that was when you and I sat down for an interview that was published in the journal *Theatre Topics*. We talked about the origins of your name, your history, how you started teaching my classes for me, how you scandalized my students with your foul mouth.

LV *[belting Céline]* It's all coming back, it's all coming back to me now.

KK *[unphased]* And since "Lessons in Drag" was the first container that held both of us together, it feels like a good title for this book, to extend the conversation.

LV But what about you?

KK What about me?

LV You interviewed *me*, back then. Now *you* need to be interviewed. How will the reader know who they're reading?

KK I mean, I've pu . . .

LV Tell me about your childhood?

KK LaWhore!

LV No seriously. You've nicely detailed who I am—a million times—but have you actually told people who Kareem is?

KK I guess not.

LV So start. *[stares in Ursula the Sea Witch]* Start!

KK Fine. *[huffs]* My name is Kareem Khubchandani. I'm a forty-two-year-old academic. I was born in Gibraltar in 1982, spent most of my childhood in Accra, Ghana. I moved to the US in 2000 for college, and while in the US I've lived in Hamilton NY, San Francisco CA, Williamstown MA, Chicago IL, Austin TX, Medford MA, and Brooklyn NY. I've also spent a substantial amount of time in Bangalore and other Indian cities after I started doing research there in 2010.

LV Wow! Mister Worldwide!

KK A Pitbull reference?

LV Are you going to pretend you don't have a crush on him?

KK *[they stare off, RuPaul versus Pearl—until Kareem gives up]* Fine. He's very hot. But my crushes are not what this conversation is supposed to be about.

LV Interview. Fine. So why do you start your biodata with all these places?

KK I don't know if the general readership will understand what biodata is, do you want to explain?

LV They have the Google. They've seen Sima Aunty and *Indian Matchmaking*. Answer my question. Why do you start your biodata with all these places?

KK I think because it signals the circuits of empire that have shaped my life path—Gibraltar, Ghana, India, all British colonies. It's what's led me to "Vagistan" as a place, a placeholder for place. It's where my need to invent place comes from.

LV Invent me?

KK That's the funny thing, I think you're constantly inventing me.

LV Ew. Too deep too fast. Leave that for *your* chapters. OK, what else?

KK I'm the author of . . .

LV Boring!

KK OK, um . . . I grew up in a Sindhi community in Ghana. Sindhis are a multi-faith ethnolinguistic community originally from Pakistan. I come from a caste of Hindu Sindhis known as *bhaibands*. Many of us are merchants. Prior to the Partition of India and Pakistan in 1947, my grandfathers were engaged in business ventures in Ghana and Gibraltar—retail, import, manufacturing. When the subcontinent was split, their families ventured from Hyderabad Sindh in Pakistan into India . . .

LV Hyderabad Sindh? Not Lahore?

KK No.

LV So . . .?

KK So . . .

LV So why is my name LaWhore?

KK Well because it's a very good pun. And because Lahore is gorgeous . . . like you.

LV Flattery will get you everywhere. [*winks*]

KK And because it diverts an easy designation of me as "Indian" so that I can live inside more complex itineraries of borders and maps. All South Asian countries are trapped in the flawed construct that is the modern nation-state, working hard to repress religious, tribal, caste, linguistic, ethnic, gender, and sexual dissidents. India in particular folds its diasporas into a murderously casteist and Islamophobic state project, and I'm not here for it. LaWhore is my way of disidentifying with these nationalisms. And, if I have to admit it, there's certainly a part of me, like many Sindhis displaced permanently into diaspora, that melancholically romanticizes imaginations of pre-Partition syncretism, that misses a Pakistan I've never been to or known. These entrenched nationalisms make the loss feel deeper.

LV You've never been to Pakistan? This is a lot. You must get in trouble for . . . appropriation?

KK I have. Some people especially don't like that I sexualize the city or the subcontinent. Eyeroll! Basically, when I went to college, and learned about histories of national and racial formations, I found myself looking for identity models that can more expansively hold my histories—South Asian, *desi*, Sindhi. Drag was an opportunity to invent a somewhere for myself. I'm not trying to appropriate Lahore or Pakistan as they are, but to find a place for myself inside fractured histories. And when it comes to Lahore, I've attempted to do my due diligence to get to know the city through books like . . .

LV Please, leave your citations for the bibliography. And also, fuck your due diligence. I end up having to be the face of your geopolitical confusion. *I'm* LaWhore.

KK Well, maybe that's one of the things you can process in this book.

LV A tall order for a short book. Speaking of geopolitical fuckery, you were telling me how your grandfathers were forced to migrate into India . . .

KK Right. Yes. But only briefly, and then eventually abroad to where their business outposts were.

LV So the men just came and scooped up the women and children and brought them to the countries where they did business?

KK I'm sure it was more complicated than that. In fact, my maternal grandfather was taken as a prisoner of war by Germany during World War II, while he was on a ship back to Sindh. And then Partition happened. He disappeared for a while. Once he was freed, he had to locate his family, which had been displaced out of Hyderabad in Pakistan to Pune in India.

LV Gibraltar? Ghana? Such random places.

KK I mean, not really. It was easier for Indian merchants to settle in these British territories. Gibraltar remains a British annex, which has made things quite complicated following Brexit since it borders Spain! Strangers are always like, you're so global, your parents must be diplomats! But it's actually this merchant-caste heritage that has propelled my family around the world.

LV So if everyone is some kind of merchant, how did you end up a professor? She's too good for the family business? She's allergic to money?

KK Oof. What are all these hard questions, Aunty? Well, our extended family business in Ghana disintegrated. And after that, for much of my life, my mother was the breadwinner, keeping us afloat. As the business crumbled, Mum witnessed how the pressure to conform to Sindhi masculinity was actually quite detrimental to the men, women, and kids around her. She didn't put it in those exact words, but she would always say, "I don't want this for you. You need to get out of here, make your own money." She didn't want the Sindhi business hustle to drain us the way it had my father and the other men around her. She wanted to break the bonds of obligation; she saw the ways that caste-based heteronormative family ties replicated unequitable forms of reciprocity. In addition to encouraging my brothers and I to find pathways out of the family business model, she would say, and this is well before I came out to her, "Never get married. Be with who you want, but don't get married." She was doing queer theory long before me, essentially linking the untenable but overlapping obligations of caste, labor, gender, and heteronormativity. This family business history, and my departure from it, has shaped a lot of my self-image. I've long imagined myself as an exception to the entrepreneurial ethos of this ethnoracial heritage . . . though maybe that's changing?

LV Oh? Are you finally leaving the academy to start your fashion line?

KK Um, I don't think those need to be mutually exclusive. But I often think about the work my mother did, the informal businesses she ran to keep us fed and in school, to offer herself travel and luxury, to provide her friends with comfort and space. I think about this alongside the work I and other drag artists do, drag labor that simultaneously entertains and convenes community. Maybe work or business don't have to be solely about individualist accumulation, or capitulate to the gendered labor expectations of caste structures. The way Mum did business brought beauty and intimacy to her work. She had to cobble together the funds to put me through college. For as much stress as this work could cause her, she had

Maybe work doesn't have to be solely about individualist accumulation, or capitulate to gender and caste norms. The way Mum did business brought beauty and intimacy to her work.

so much fun doing it: sketching designs, curating Pinterest boards, shopping for textiles. I know she wanted a different future for my brothers and I, but I don't think she realized that she was already modeling that something else—"intimate economies" that offer a different way to provide services, to buy and sell, to earn and circulate money.

LV And so I repeat, are you leaving the academy to start your fashion line?

KK [*grimaces*] Who knows? I like the steady income of being an academic, I like the structure of teaching and researching. But I also have the model of Mum's hustle, one that allowed her to live a better life and to make life better for other women as well. The way she conducted business, from the home, over a cup of tea, made work feel less transactional, more intimate. Amidst having steady work, I miss and reminisce about the intimate and informal work Mum did. I *do* dream of a future in fashion. I've been institutionally bound for so long—I went from undergrad to working in student affairs, to a PhD, to a postdoc, to a tenure-track job. They've provided steadiness of income and status while living on visas in the US.

LV But you *do* work beyond the academy. You do drag!

KK True. But my performance gigs are often on college campuses, and I feel the friction between everyday academic work and the nightclub hustle when I do college shows. I feel so gauche, overexplaining to colleagues who invite me to perform at their university why I'm not simply charging a baseline academic speaker fee. On top of that, I get embarrassed for what feel like excessive requests for an academic event: appropriate publicity, powerful sound, theatrical lighting!

LV Yes! The lighting! Warm front lighting! Most important!

KK You get it! And you're right, beyond this tenured gig, drag reminds me what it means to hustle, the way Mum did, to make it work, to work intimately with others, to turn my body into a business.

LV [*singing*] She's a hustler baby . . .

KK Jokes? Right when I'm being vulnerable?

LV [*glibly*] Vulnerability is overrated.

KK For once we agree.

LV Meaning?

KK You're the one who said it.

LV Ya, I'm a stunning and cunty drag queen. I can say whatever I feel like and keep going. But you're an academic, you're not allowed to just make offhand comments about major cultural terminologies. What do *you* mean, "vulnerability is overrated"?

KK [*stunned, he gathers himself*] OK, fine. I think "vulnerability" has come to refer to a practice of using personal narrative, particularly stories of loss and trauma, as a device to get people to trust you as an authentic speaker. No doubt, there is gorgeous and urgent art and theory that come out of personal experience, but there's also danger there. Liberal publics have been trained to empathetically listen to personal narrative as the most convincing form of "data"—and that absolves them of thinking more carefully about historical, institutional, political, and systemic forms of power and violence. The narrative becomes about individual resilience, heroism, and genius. So when we obfuscate systems and structures, we absolve audiences of their complicity, power, and privilege. This then places pressure on activists, writers, and artists to invest in first-person narratives, particularly trauma narratives, as the best or maybe even the only way to comment on sociopolitical conditions. This lands us in a place where spilling your guts to an audience of strangers who have no accountability to you counts as "healing."

LV So, Professor, what are readers supposed to do with *this* book? Which is [*checks notes on imaginary clipboard*] *literally* about your experiences?

KK Good question, Aunty! Gooooood question. I'm hoping they won't read my reflections about my life and my career for insights into me as an individual. I don't need them to feel close to *me* at the end. Rather I hope we give readers tools to get closer to themselves, and the people and worlds that matter to them most. I really hope no one comes here in search of my wounds and trauma and brokenness. Rather, I want to offer drag, as I know it, to others because it is a vibrant resource with which to hone a relationship to the rest of the world, to center embodiment and reciprocity in increasingly alienated and automated neoliberal conditions—whether in the academy or beyond. What I think I'm doing is using personal experience to illuminate patterns and problems that we all participate in—and point out the ways that drag might offer us some tools to respond to them.

> Drag is a vibrant resource with which to hone a relationship to the rest of the world, to center embodiment and reciprocity—whether in the academy or beyond.

LV OK, that was [*stifles yawn*] satisfactory.

KK Ma'am. I wasn't looking for approval.

LV Fine. I *was* being a bitch. But I get where you're coming from. My show *Lessons in Drag w/ LaWhore Vagistan* definitely invites the audience into a shared experience, but I'm not doing it with the trauma shrauma gag. The show works without being *about me*.

KK It's about me!

LV You got me, gal! It's about *you*. It's about your scholarship and research, but not your life experiences. Nor mine. I don't think we necessarily need to rely on personal narrative as the foundation for intimacy.

KK Can you back up for a second and explain what *Lessons in Drag*—the show—is?

LV Wow. Such good pedagogy. Really looking out for the reader.

[*adjusts her seating posture, as if she's on a talk show, playing to the studio audience—it's almost as if she's given this speech before*] *Lessons in Drag* gives the "lesson" a drag makeover. It's a ninety-minute show that I perform primarily on college campuses, and it restyles the academic lecture as a drag show. It makes learning a nightlife event, even when some campuses schedule me for 5 p.m.! V homophobic! [*relaxes out of the Wendy Williams demeanor and talks to Kareem again*] In the show, I'll take ideas from your research—and other peoples' too—like accents, or aunties, or appropriation, and turn them into lip-synch numbers. So I'll go directly from lecturing about the disciplining of Indian accents as a consequence of neoliberal globalization to lip-synching Gaga's "Telephone" alongside the voices of call center workers. T-T-T-Telephone. Or I'll drop into Disney ballads as a way of explaining orientalism and disidentification. Help the audience see a [*holds up right thumb and pointer finger in an O*] "hole" new world. It is a veritable sissification of the academic lecture. There are slides, citations, and Q&A, but there are also costume reveals, wig changes, confetti, dance-alongs, multiple songs by Fergie, and a lot of dick jokes. Full drag show!

KK Yes! Full drag show. But also full lesson. Which is always my takeaway from the show: that drag is very much a site of learning! Drag artists are potent teachers. When I attend shows, I learn so much. I learn queer history and local gay gossip. There are so many new words used on the drag stage to learn.

LV Slay, yaaaaas, werk.

KK Exactly. Also important to remember that this queer language primarily emerges from Black queer communities before filtering into mainstream gay spaces. Truly, clubs are classrooms, especially themed drag shows! They are master classes in adaptation! I don't know if you remember, but *NoFilter*'s "Myth Thing" milked the antics of Greek and Roman gods for their perverse drama. And *Fagtasia*'s "Hobbitfest" twisted Tolkien into an erotic trans romp. Linda Hutcheon would have gagged!

LV Linda who? Is she a drag queen?

KK Sorry, academic joke. But she might as well be. She's probably turned a lot of people gay. But drag shows truly are where genres and tastes collide. They often become their very own comparative literature classes. Bertha Vanayshun's *Drag History Hour* show covers everything from pirates to the Harlem Renaissance. Cunning Stunt offered a literal PowerPoint lecture on the history of the rainbow flag at his Pride 2024 show. At *Holy Hole*, Sherman taught the audience about every possible trans and nonbinary figure in the Christian canon. Beyond the shows themselves, drag artists function as the resident historians of our collective spaces. I imagine you'll still be performing on drag stages, even when I'm too old to tolerate the chaos of the club dance floor.

LV Yes! Shower me with compliments!

KK Truly, I'm grateful for how you put my scholarship in drag. You dress it up. Or maybe undress it, stripping off all the constraining garments of industry-specific jargon and stuffy scholarly prose. My education in the Northwestern University tradition of Performance Studies taught me that performance can be understood as a medium for staging research, much like academic lectures or published essays. One is not more effective than the other. Rather, they accomplish different things, reach people in different ways, teach people through alternative channels.

LV So this is a thing? I'm not the only one who takes research and turns it into performance?

KK Definitely not the only one! I was lucky to have models for this kind of work when I was a grad student: D. Soyini Madison choreographed her research on environmental activism in Ghana into a play titled "Water Rites," and E. Patrick Johnson based his play "Pouring Tea: Black Gay Men of the South Tell Their Tales" on his book *Sweet Tea: Black Gay Men of the South—*

An Oral History. The show *Lessons in Drag* brings to life pieces of my research that didn't fully shine in writing, or that never made it into my writing at all.

LV Do you remember where this all started?

KK Oh god.

BOTH *Material Boy*!

LV You explain.

KK No, please, you.

LV Oh god, don't make me say it. This book was your idea.

KK Fine. So *Material Boy* was my first ever "solo show."

LV Solo show! [*cackles maniacally*]

KK Listen. (A), Your show, *Lessons in Drag*, is also a "solo show." And (B), I get that the "solo show" is a rite of passage for budding performance artists that we look back on with embarrassment. But it was transformative for me. It was the very first time I took full artistic control of something, from concept to execution.

LV Sweet little baby.

KK Can I tell you a secret?

LV Only if you're OK with me telling everyone else. [*smiles that churail smile*]

KK I fully expect you to, gossip queen! When people ask when I first started doing drag, my party line is that I began in the summer of 2009 at a fundraiser called *Jai Ho!* for the queer South Asian nonprofit Trikone-Chicago. That was certainly the first time I performed in a nightclub. But our debut was actually a few months earlier.

LV I love how you're telling me this like I don't already know.

KK For the public, LaWhore! Not everyone was there. At the time I was in a PhD program in Performance Studies at Northwestern University, where we were invited—required—to create a "recital," a performance that responded to a research question. I cobbled together a twenty-five-minute solo show that toyed with masculine and feminine drag, onstage performance and backstage monologues, and memorized texts from queer South Asian diasporic novelists. The show, *Material Boy*, was responding to the question: "Can the veil be an alternative metaphor to the closet for diasporic people called to perform their identity by multiple nation states?"

LV Ooooooooo.

KK No "ooo!" Ewwwwww. It was very cringe. In general, I'm OK with being a little bit cringey, but to talk about this you need to buy me a few tequilas. Following the recital, I would perform excerpts of *Material Boy* at graduate student conferences and activist events, while also building a larger repertoire of nightclub performances. And then you and I published our interview. That's when *Material Boy* morphed into the show *Lessons in Drag w/ LaWhore Vagistan*.

LV So you're OK with people knowing my *real* origin story.

KK Yes. I think it's actually quite important to know that LaWhore Vagistan was conceived by a very zealous humanities grad student. From the scholarly and literary discourses of diaspora, Partition, migration, racism, displacement, nostalgia, mimicry, and subversion. From *Terrorist Assemblages, Global Divas, Impossible Desires, Appropriating Blackness, Disidentifications, The Black Atlantic*. From *The Buddha of Suburbia, Ode to Lata, Funny Boy*, and *Blue Boy*. What I hadn't anticipated was that once you stepped out of the academy and into the nightclub, you would continue to shape my intellectual inquiries. *Jai Ho!*, the party you hosted—a party that has run for over fifteen years—became one of the primary field sites

> **LaWhore Vagistan was conceived by a very zealous humanities grad student, from the scholarly and literary discourses of diaspora, partition, migration, racism, displacement, nostalgia, mimicry, and subversion.**

for my first book *Ishtyle: Accenting Gay Indian Nightlife*. Moving through the world with the notoriety of a drag queen has fundamentally shaped my research data and the way I analyze it. You showed up in every aspect of my work life.

LV Wait. How did we get here? I thought I was supposed to be explaining what the *Lessons in Drag* show was.

KK Sorry. I got carried away. Sometimes it's like we share a mind! You were talking about how the show is not about staging yourself and your story.

LV Yes, exactly. But this is where I think your critique of vulnerability might be a little short-sighted. You're too focused on trauma and personal narrative as the only way to connect with others.

KK Means?

LV In my experience, a lot of people *fall* into my show because they see my body working on stage, sweating and breathing heavily into the mic after dancing. There are other ways to reveal oneself to the public that are not about exposing the inner dimension of the psyche, but about presence, making intention and labor visible and visceral. I feel like when people see or feel the work that I've put in—whether it's my look, or my lesson plan, or my lip-synch—they're ready to be there with me. I'm there to work, so they stay to work too. To participate, to root for me, to get involved. There's a safety and comfort that comes from laughing, and breathing, and learning together. There are ways of baring yourself—your politics, your ideas, your body—that aren't about using trauma as a conduit for connection.

KK Fair. LaWhore, I always forget how smart you are. I guess I just want to be cautious about how you and I commodify ourselves, how we make ourselves available to others. There are so many traps, so many ways we can be cannibalized as minoritarian people, given the limited frameworks through which we can be legible in the public sphere.

LV I hear you, Mister Big Words.

KK Um, Professor Big Words? I have tenure.

LV Ew. Jesus. Gross. But I still think we can still make room for generous connections with others, even with strangers, through laughter and beauty and pleasure.

KK How did we get onto this vulnerability stuff anyways?

LV Oh. Ya. You were talking about why you did or didn't want to follow the Sindhi business path . . .

KK One hell of a detour. The point I was getting to is that when it comes to thinking I'm on the outside of Sindhi business circuits and I'm doing something a little less selfish, less capitalistic, by being a teacher, I'm forced to reckon with the fact that universities are corporations. I'm not on the outside of capitalism as a professor. [*breathes deeply*] This is not some big new revelation. So many brilliant colleagues working in Critical University Studies have argued that neoliberalism corrals even the most radical and interdisciplinary corners of the academy into its agenda, engendering an amnesia of their activist pasts. But experiencing it all as a faculty member has been wild. It's hit me quite hard. [*scooches forward in his seat*] From the domestication of Black Lives Matter activism into DEI committees, to the vicious repression of pro-Palestine activism on all our campuses, to the readiness of university administrations to comply with rollbacks on academic freedom, it's evident that most universities are way more interested in appeasing donors and mollifying critics than creating an equitable learning environment for their students. [*leaning forward, barely even sitting on the*

By being a teacher, I'm forced to reckon with the fact that universities are corporations. I'm not on the outside of capitalism as a professor.

chair anymore] They would rather sanitize demands for justice with trite gestures to free speech and safety, than fight for truly liberatory futures for those who are most subjugated. I've watched universities renege on the promises they made in the wake of Black Lives Matter organizing to decarcerate their campuses, and instead call in the police to arrest Black, brown, and Jewish students for opposing the genocide in Gaza. It's dystopia. [*sinks back into seat*]

LV OK, go off Professor! [*snap! snap! snap!*] Yas! [*to the tune of Rihanna's "Disturbia"*] Your mind's in dystopia! [*comes back to earth*] Now what else should readers of your book—our book—know about you? What do you look like?

KK After all this, you're going to make me write a Grindr profile?

LV Ya babes. Work through the trauma. You said it yourself: it's what readers expect! How else will they know they can trust you? [*mimics the Grindr notification sound*] Prrrrrt. [*cackles*]

KK [*glares in sad homosexual*] Ew. Fine. I'm five-six tall, brown skinned, hairy. Very hairy. Wavy black-gray hair. Skin-fade on the sides. I usually keep a beard, except when I'm doing drag. I like to wear short shorts and loose-fitting shirts . . . showing off the assets people compliment the most and hiding the others that incur direct judgment. [*pauses, looking for the right words*] I don't hate having a belly, but I am conscious of the way that it makes me appear to others as the wrong kind of urban subject: unhealthy, undisciplined, excessive.

LV Fuck them! Fuck the racist, ableist, anti-fat fuckers!

KK Yes. Um. Fuck them! You always help me find the right words, Aunty! I also love wearing overflowing garments: pallazos, saris, caftans . . .

LV [*quoting herself, singing*] 'Cuz I look best, when I'm dressed like an aunty.

KK [*laughs diplomatically*] Colors, prints, patterns, elaborate weaves. Yes, very aunty looks. We have that in common. But I think again it excludes me from a certain realm of proper masculinity, the type that's considered professional, desirable, reliable, rational, authoritative, athletic. And then you throw in my faggy voice. Every telemarketer refers to me as "ma'am" when I pick up the phone. And my bouncy walk. Just so gay all the time.

I'm not always received as a man worth respecting—or even as a "man" at all. Not that I'm invested in being a man per se; I aspire to aunty-ness.

LV And why does your reader need to know this?

KK You made me tell them.

LV [*stares in Simi Garewal, crosses legs in Sharon Stone*]

KK Well, I think because I certainly enjoy some of the unearned benefits that come with masculinity, caste privilege, and able-bodiedness in the university. But I don't experience masculinity in some kind of uniform way within institutional *or* social spaces. I'm not always received as a man worth respecting—or even as a "man" at all. Not that I'm invested in being a man per se; I aspire to aunty-ness more than anything else. But in professional and social spaces, I'm small and brown and overdressed. And—in the way that people of color have regularly been infantilized under colonial regimes—I'm treated as cute and adorable and fancy, but not afforded seriousness.

LV And you think *I'm* taken seriously?

KK I mean, have you seen how people treat you? They'll open the door for you. They'll buy you drinks. They'll dote on you. I can barely convince my students to call me doctor or professor, but they'll refer to you as Dr. Vagistan all semester long.

LV And it's because . . .

KK [*evangelizing*] You are powerful. Drag has acquired power. It demands admiration. It commands . . . in nightclub spaces *and* in the classroom. And you're sparkling in sequins. You're a full foot taller than me, because heels plus wig. In the very spaces where you become a goddess and icon, I feel very small. [*breathless*]

LV [*shows genuine emotion for the first time in her life*] Kareem . . .

KK . . . and that's fine. Because I have you when I need to feel otherwise.

LV [*back to her bully self*] So you admit, you like doing drag?

KK I don't know whether "liking" doing drag is really the word I'd go for. But I'm very aware of how much of a thrill it gives me to feel important and fabulous on stage, to simply feel valued. I know it has shaped my career. I know how much it has taught me, how much it enables me to teach others. In fact, that's why I want us to write this book. *Lessons in Drag* is supposed to be as much about what academia does for drag as it is about what drag does for academia.

LV I need to be blunt, Mister—sorry, Professor Academic. You open your first book with "I fucking love drag queens!" But what is your resistance to just saying "I love doing drag"?

KK Because it's hard, Dr. Vagistan. It's where I experience the most imposter syndrome. On stage, I feel powerful and fabulous, but then I see the photo or video of a performance, and I'm disappointed by my own mediocrity. Just fine at staging femininity, while also barely successful at being masculine.

LV So why keep doing it?

KK Because that's how colonial binary gender systems are supposed to work! Gender is always unfinished business, and the insufficiency we feel in keeping up with idealized norms keeps us compliant with patriarchy, with capitalism. Sure, theory has taught me this. But drag, drag renders this dilemma material. It forces

Drag has kept me grounded as a scholar, assuring me that my body is of the utmost importance even as I pursue "a life of the mind."

me to do the hard work of being with my body and its contradictions, and you know I prefer to be lazy. Drag requires me to work *with* gender rather than letting gender just happen to me, and this is a gift, an exhausting but life-giving gift. Drag has pushed me past my mundane insecurities to think and learn and try harder. To fantasize, to acquire new skills, for the stage and the everyday. This artform has left a deep imprint on me as a researcher and a teacher. Drag has kept me grounded as a scholar, assuring me that my body is of the utmost importance even as I pursue "a life of the mind." Drag has led me to new and specific research questions that were never on my agenda. Drag has become a *way* of asking questions and investigating inquiries. Drag has taught me other ways to impart knowledge and initiate difficult conversations, in the classroom and beyond. Which is why I—we—need to write this book.

LV But Professor, didn't you *just* write a book about drag?

KK Why are you always coming with the reads, Aunty? Yes, yes I did. *Decolonize Drag* was my humble attempt to contribute to the fabulous body of scholarship on drag that teaches us about gender as a social construct bound to race, how lipsynch creates new meaning, how drag artists invoke histories of power through dress. But in addition to the study of drag, I want to consider what drag does to study. How can drag transform our research agendas, writing practices, and pedagogy?

LV Then tell me about *this* book.

KK OK, here's the pitch. *Lessons in Drag* is a study of the relationship between pedagogy and drag. What does being a professor teach a drag queen about her craft, and what does being a drag queen teach a professor about his craft?

What does being a professor teach a drag queen about craft, and what does being a drag queen teach a professor about craft?

LV And you think people who are not professors or drag artists will care about any of this? Who is interested in *both* drag and education?

KK Well first off there are *many* drag PhDs!

LV Excuse me? *I* am not the only one?

KK LOL Aunty! No, absolutely not! E. Patrick Johnson is Shenita Bath. Lawrence La Fountain-Stokes is Lola von Miramar. Ryan Persadie is Tifa Wine. Qais Munhazim is Tal Eebani. Enzo Toral is Penelope Sumac. John Musser is Veronica Bleaus. Mike Atienza is Ma. Arte. Nino Testa is Maria von Clapp. Jacob Bird is Dinah Lux. Uzma Zafar is Sher. Ryan Ashley Caldwell is Sister Electra-Complex. Payne Banister is Matilda Rose. Gabriel Dharmoo is Bijuriya. Harris Kornstein is Lil Miss Hot Mess. Mark Montondo is Ms. Golden Delicious. Adrienne Huard is Randy River. Bimbola Akinbola is Mars Violet Basqui'not. Jo Rezes is Susan Skintag. Javier Hurtado is Perra Pumps. Shaka McGlotten is Jed(i)mmanence X. Mark Edward is Gale Force.

LV And I thought I was special. OK, so like twenty people will relate.

KK You're pigeonholing drag, setting it up as a niche practice for a select group of people who are over-confident—even perhaps delusional.

LV Clocked! [*Alyssa Edwards tongue pop*]

KK In a way, though, we're all participating in drag all the time. That's Gender Studies 101. But scholars have arrived at this foundational argument through a kind of theoretical engagement with drag, the idea of drag, not necessarily a material study of drag artists. But if we actually do drag—engage the process of assembling a persona, a performance, a body; find one's footing in nightlife and activist communities; develop relationships with mentors; build wardrobes; craft digital and "embodied avatars"—we can arrive at drag's concrete and instructive offerings. Drag, simultaneously bold and intricate in its craft, has helped me rethink rigor beyond its white and western empiricist tendencies. Reading, writing, research can be incredibly lonely work in which we potentially lose our relationship to the world, we lose our bodies in pursuit of intellectual investigation and lifestyles not necessarily designed with our well-being in mind. Drag can keep us accountable to our community, to our interlocutors, to ourselves—at least it has for me.

LV Wow. Is the academy that fucked up?

KK It can be. But so is the drag scene! Right? Obsessed with whiteness, perfection, competition, gatekeeping. But here's what gets me. [*suddenly serving Annalise Keating*] Why are we so seldom invited to think about the club and the classroom together? Drag, and trans life more generally, is coming under greater attack by the state at the same time as universities are being censored for the knowledge we produce about minoritarian life. The right sees both of these spaces as dangerous sites of knowledge production—shouldn't we take that as our cue to think them together? Neither is a perfect ecology, but I'm ready to ask what they can offer each other. To me, the promise of drag has always been performance, the craft of seizing control over how we use our bodies and the aesthetics that surround us to reflect the world back to itself. Or to conjure a world we wish could exist. Isn't that what a classroom should be? Sometimes that goes according to plan; sometimes it fails; and sometimes it unexpectedly becomes something else altogether, something we didn't know we wanted or needed. Drag is one way of tapping into that possibility of emplacement, of worldmaking.

LV Go. Off. Professor. Teach me! I'm excited now. [*lips pursed à la Jennifer Coolidge.*] You make me wanna write this book real bad. And we'll co-write the chapters?

KK I was thinking we'll alternate chapters.

LV OMG. But like, what am I going to write?

KK We can take it one at a time. I definitely want to connect drag to research, teaching, and writing, but you can feel free to play it by ear.

LV Do I have to write like an academic journal article? Like thesis, lit review, method, citations, and whatnot?

KK I mean, you *know* how to do that. But you don't have to. I'm thinking of each chapter as a lesson, a "How to . . ." in which we distill our experiences and observations into transferable practices. Memoir plus manual.

LV Memoir plus manual. Like those stupid online recipes that force you to read someone's life history before they tell you what the ingredients are in a three-cheese quesadilla? It's three cheeses and a tortilla, Agatha. I don't need to know how your lactose intolerance disappeared after your divorce. But I *do* want to know why you got divorced?! OK, now I'm starving. Do you think they serve quesadillas here?

KK Oh my god. LaWhore. Focus. No, not like that. But maybe kind of like that? Yes, people will have to parse through our biographies to arrive at the takeaways. But I'm hoping that our narratives will really help lead to the claims we want to make. And I'm hoping that by spending time with your experiences, the reader gets to linger in your beauty and brilliance.

LV Well, when you put it that way . . .

KK Are you in?

LV I'm in.

KK I love it!

LV How much do I get paid?

KK [*getting up to go*] Sorry, what did you say . . . ?

LV How much do I get paid? [*sound of footsteps, door closing*] Kareem?

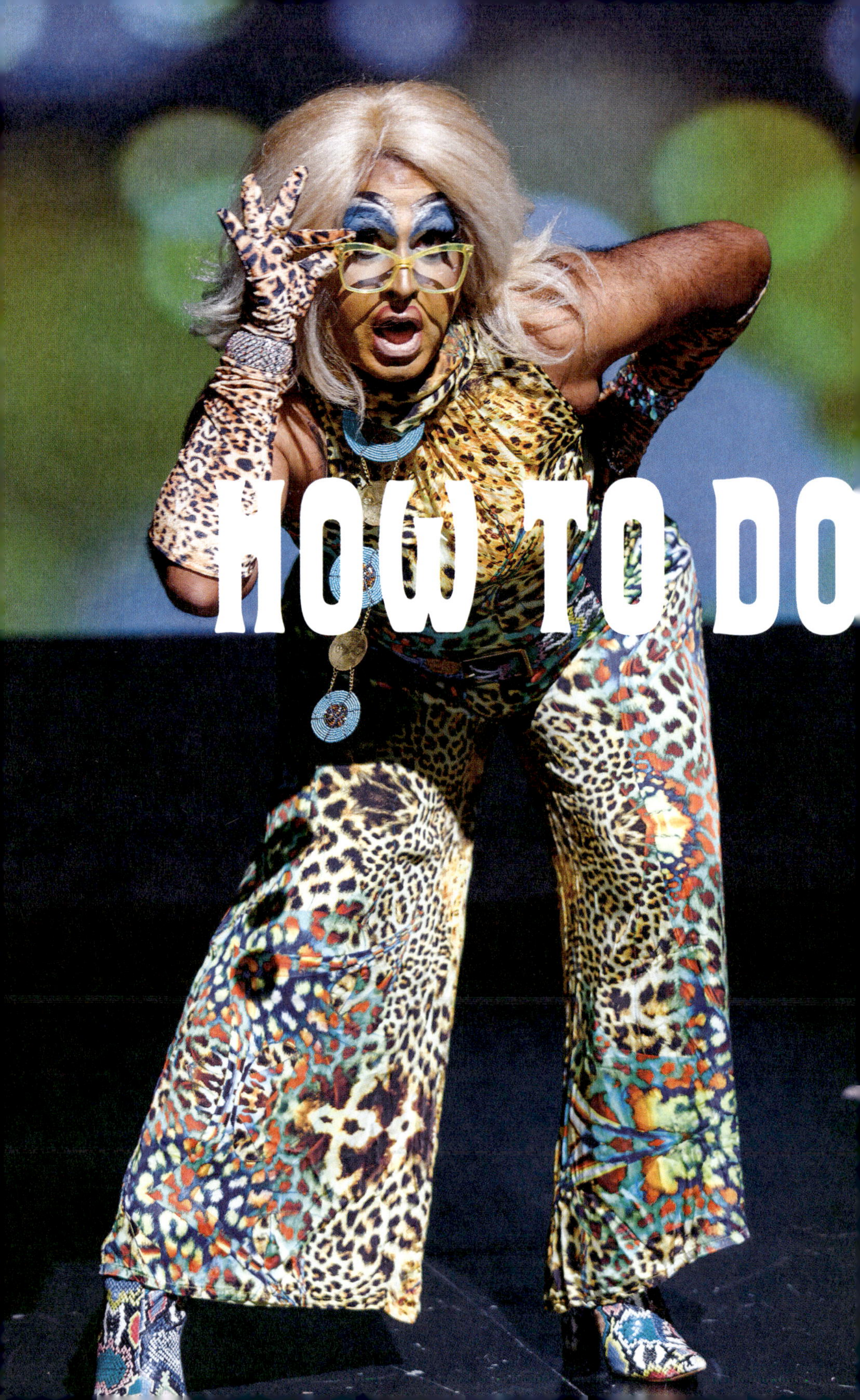

HOW TO DO

RESEARCH

Drag has changed my life.

I performed in drag at a nightclub for the first time in Chicago when I was twenty-six years old. I was a naïve and eager gay boy, feeling fabulous, living in a large US city for the first time. That performance was meant to be a one-time show for a one-off fundraiser, a mere hobby as I tried to make new friends in a new city. If you had told me that July that in the near future my closets would be overflowing with saris and sequins and that my bookshelves would be repurposed for wigs; that weeknights would be spent bedazzling Swiffers and sacred sleep-in Saturday mornings would be given over to hosting drag brunch; that I would make be making music videos, giving TEDx talks, hosting queer parties in Delhi and Bombay and Fire Island and Bushwick; that I would be officiating weddings and memorial services in drag, and even performing at celebrity birthday parties; that I would be invited to share the stage with *RuPaul's Drag Race* winners like Sasha Velour, Nymphia Wind, and Raja . . . I would probably have believed you!

> Drag has lightened the work of scholarly inquiry, teaching me the value of play and creativity in writing, teaching, publishing, and lecturing.

I never explicitly wanted to be a drag queen, but I've always had an appetite for the limelight.

It's the less spectacular pieces of the story I probably could not have predicted. Like waking up at 6 a.m. on a Tuesday to do my makeup in order to teach my undergraduate classes. Or being invited *in drag* to speak at Area Studies conferences and at Christian universities. Or publishing interviews in scholarly journals with LaWhore Vagistan—that is to say, *with myself*. Or coining "Critical Aunty Studies" as a field of study. Drag has transformed my career in ways that I could never have prepared for. It has lightened the work of scholarly inquiry, teaching me the value of play and creativity in writing, teaching, publishing, and lecturing.

Drag turned research into a deeply physical practice. And this form of research has transformed me, my body, my psyche, my work, my life. Research has made me a drag queen, a diva, and an aunty. Being a drag queen, diva, and aunty has, in turn, shaped my research.

COMING TO ACADEMIA

I applied to graduate school because I heard that "a PhD pays for itself." As a first-generation college student, it took a while to understand how universities work. I moved from Accra, Ghana, to central New York state in 2000 to attend Colgate University. Over the course of four years, I drifted from the hard to the social sciences, from chemistry to sociology and anthropology. I was seduced into the field by Yamuna Sangarasivam, a brilliant scholar whose fieldwork on Tamil resistance movements in ethno-nationalist Sri Lanka reordered my understanding of gender, race, violence, and research method. The critical lens with which to study culture that she and others in the department offered helped me make sense of my experiences as a recent migrant, my nascent queerness, and the local and global violence that followed the September 2001 attack on the Twin Towers. I decided to major in a field of study that I had never even heard of prior to coming to university. Ah, the power of a liberal arts education!

My financial aid package at Colgate covered two-thirds of my tuition and board, and my mother scrounged and struggled to pay the rest. In order to have liquid cash of my own, I worked in the Office of Student Activities. I loved that job! I loved learning about how money moved within the university, about where decision-making powers lived. When I graduated, I applied for positions in student affairs, especially those in search of "multicultural" expertise—in these job applications I was able to leverage both my sociology and anthropology bachelors and my student affairs work experience.

In my four subsequent years working at Williams College I was exposed to the guts of the university, attending deans' meetings and sitting on committees. No longer a student, but still in a college town, I became friendly with professors and learned about their paths to the PhD. These friends and colleagues made the grad school experience transparent, looked over my application essays, and teased out what I should look for in an acceptance package. I finally understood what people meant when they said, "A PhD pays for itself." It wasn't free education per se; it involved providing cheap labor to the university as a teaching or research assistant. OK, so grad school wasn't free, but it was a ticket out of that job and town I was stagnating in. It was a chance to be curious and experimental once again.

Like sociology and anthropology, performance studies was a discipline I learned about mere months before committing to it. Performance studies centers performance as an object of research (the thing you study), as an analytic (attending to things that aren't always called performance

Drag, while initially just the object of my research, became a research method.

as performance), as a research method (you gather and process data through performance, participation, and embodied interpretation), as a way of presenting research (shows like *Water Rites*, *Sweet Tea*, and *Lessons in Drag*), and as a pedagogical tool (embodied exercises in the classroom, whether reading things out loud or creating embodied tableaus from text as a mode of interpretation). In this chapter I focus on how drag, while initially just the object of my research, became a research method. I also show how doing drag raised new research questions for me in grad school and beyond that weren't already on my research agenda. And finally I think about how drag became a crucial way of staging my research. For those not reading this chapter as researchers or academics, I hope this narrative offers you a glimpse into how drag works as a centrifugal force pulling knowledge and meaning in toward itself so that it becomes both a relational practice and a key lens to understand power and difference.

DRAG ETHNOGRAPHER

I enrolled in a PhD program with the hopes of conducting an ethnographic research project on drag. Instead of writing about the spectacular artistry on stage, however, I became a drag queen ethnographer who wrote about her adoring public, the beautiful queers on the dance floor, and their mundane but urgent acts of creativity. Drag turned me around, quite literally, to think more expansively about where performance happens in nightlife spaces.

I was seduced by drag early on in my queer nightlife journey. During my first years in the US, I would ride a seven-hour bus from my small college town to New York City to attend *Desilicious* parties, quarterly queer nights that featured Bollywood music, a queer South Asian crowd, and fierce drag. They were a valuable respite from the heteronormativity and whiteness of the rural northeast. I was vigilant not to miss the queens' performances, especially because their show times were never announced. I was enamored by their mystery: their sudden appearance on stage, their masterful enactments of film choreography, and then their disappearance into the forest of bodies. My graduate school applications promised a study of these dancers.

When I moved to Chicago in the fall of 2008 to begin my PhD at Northwestern, there was no queer desi nightlife scene there. And when I returned to New York from Chicago to visit *Desilicious* again, I learned that the queens I loved in my college years didn't perform regularly anymore. This dearth of drag did many things to shape *Ishtyle*. It required me to take my gaze away from spectacular stages and pay attention to all the other "performances" that happen in nightlife spaces: dance gestures, spatial configurations, clothing choices, speech acts, flirtations. My fieldwork in Chicago and Bangalore led me to write a nightlife ethnography about queer middle-class Indian migrant workers. I focused on their micro performances of dress, speech, and social dance in clubs and at parties as acts of value making.

In *Ishtyle*, I certainly appear in the text but I don't think of it as autoethnographic. This text was not *about* me, even if I did experience the complexities of gender, migration, and desire in ways similar to my interlocutors. I made it my obligation to tell my interlocutors' stories first. But performing as LaWhore Vagistan had everything to do with who was willing to talk with me—and what they wanted to talk with me about.

LaWhore Vagistan made her nightclub debut in the summer of 2009 at *Jai Ho!*, a queer Bollywood night raising funds for a newly formed queer South Asian organization, Trikone-Chicago. Despite my unpolished presentation, or perhaps because of it, the *Jai Ho!* audience was enthusiastic for more LaWhore. I did drag, not out of any deep or long-standing desire to indulge in feminine embodiment, but because I thought it necessary for the fundraiser's success. The fundraiser continued to happen, so I continued to perform.

Jai Ho! developed into a quarterly party and into one of my research sites. The typical expectation of a researcher is that she does not influence or shape the site that she studies. In my case, I literally created the site. That doesn't mean that I knew what would happen, or how. No matter how much influence I had in crafting that vital queer brown space, there was still so much to learn about it, so much unpredictability in that room of strangers dancing. Reflexive anthropology had taught me that the ethnographer must account for her presence in the field, but I hadn't actively anticipated what that would look like for me, until I did drag. My embodied involvement in Trikone-Chicago didn't by any means compromise my study. Rather, by refusing the detachment expected of the researcher, I found myself better equipped to account for *how* I knew the things I knew.

> Performing as LaWhore Vagistan had everything to do with who was willing to talk with me—and what they wanted to talk with me about.

Performing as LaWhore shaped the content of my ethnographic research because she elicited *more* performance from my interlocutors. Witnessing my drag show provided the audience opportunities both to respond to my performance and to stage *their own* cultural affinities: circling money around my body in praise before tucking it into my waist like a wealthy uncle, sliding imaginary thousand-rupee notes off their palms toward me like a Kollywood villain. Watching one video back, I see LaWhore bringing her hands into a prayer position as a thank you for a tip. "Namaste hands" are an orientalizing gesture I avoid when performing. However, the *way* LaWhore was hailed by an audience member—he circled his hands around my temples and then drew his knuckles to the sides of his face, removing the evil eye from me like my aunties used to—sent me back in time to a preteen version of me, who responded to everything with namastes. In the adrenaline-fueled fog of performance, I'd forgotten to archive this uncharacteristic moment in my memory. But seeing it captured on video reveals to me how drag—interactive, proximal, and improvised—happens *between* bodies and not alone on stage. It brings out more than I prepared for; it brings out more than I knew was already there.

My drag invited embodied responses from partygoers, which offered other ways of understanding what forms of knowledge were in the space. While I performed "Chane Ke Khet Mein," I heard Amit jealously claim, "That's my song!" Sunny squeezed his little body through the crowd to play Salman Khan to my Malaika Arora. Up there on the stage, I watched Raja mouth along to "Nakka Mukka." A native Tamil speaker, his lip-synch was so much sharper than mine. Next time you're at a live drag show, try looking away from the stage. Watch that one audience member, enjoying the anonymity of all eyes being on the stage, take the queen's permission to feel his fiercest fantasy. So much drag is happening off-stage.

The reason I could take in all these *other* performances was because of my location in the club, on the stage. We experience the world from where we are and how we move through it, not just metaphorically, socially, or politically, but physically too. Where we're standing when we experience something affects how we experience it; we have access to an entirely different set of information than someone standing somewhere else. With this awareness, we can make informed interpretations of our data. Doing research as a drag queen physically reoriented my position in the club, requiring me to look outward from the stage, to look at audiences as performers.

Stages become the default focal point of the night if we don't wrench our gaze away from them. When I taught a Queer Nightlife graduate seminar at the University of Texas at Austin in 2015, I took my students to a gay club. Each student was designated to take notes on a different aspect of the night: fashion and style, architecture and lighting, inter-

Doing research as a drag queen physically reoriented my position in the club, requiring me to look outward from the stage, to look at audiences as performers.

actions between staff and patrons, social dance, the drag show. During the drag show, one queen performed a rather upsetting number that made light of intergenerational sexual violence. This performance became the center of *every* student's response paper. *All* their other data fell away because of this one moment. The stage provides a common experience of the night. In *Ishtyle*, I argue how important the drag show is in welcoming, grounding, situating strangers in the nightclub. As it becomes an orienting device, it ends up providing *the* most substantive part of research documentation, despite the fact that interesting things are happening everywhere else as well.

But what changes when you, the researcher, are the one on stage? Standing up on my makeshift stage at *Jai Ho!*—a narrow bench that ran along the side of the bar—I was able to see the club's makeup and layout. I could observe clearly how dancers were clumped, or in circles, or facing me. Being on stage taught me that some party patrons were not there to watch me at all, despite the draw of the stage. On stage, I make it a point to make eye contact with audience members across the room, a tried-and-true performance technique to get people to share the moment with you. But I would see that many were much more interested in making out with each other or jostling at the bar for drinks. The gall! My vantage point gave me perspective on the many and messy desires of the crowd, the ones that are harder to see when you're in the thick of it all.

Other nightlife researchers offer perspectives on perspective. Karen Jaime describes how her work as a bouncer at Double-Headed Disco in New York, at the threshold of the club, gave her tools to theorize the political economies that structure desire and pleasure inside *and* outside the space. When Joe Parslow documents their work as a drag show producer alongside their analysis of these shows, they teach us how to view drag from the side, to go beyond the frontal view and immediate action of the

My vantage point gave me perspective on the many and messy desires of the crowd.

show, and to witness the lengthy labor and backstage antics that animate London's drag scene. For me, performing in the club, working the door, and circulating after the show made me an object of attention—people would come up to *me* and tell me what they thought of me, of the show, of the night. Once, as I arrived at *Jai Ho!*, Raja asked, "Can we go in the back? I want to retie your sari. I learned in Bombay, at house parties. My sisters showed me." This was one of many moments in which LaWhore, the drag queen, and not Kareem, the graduate student, elicited connection and insight. Raja's offer shed light onto the transnational routes of aesthetics, the bonds of chosen kinship that keep queer people alive, and the many ways of being sexy beyond western club style and normative Indian sari drapes that are associated with respectable femininity.

Since I had *just* started doing drag, I was especially reflexive about my relationship to femininity.

It's become very apparent to me that there are many things Kareem wouldn't have learned about the *Jai Ho!* partygoers, had LaWhore not been the event's resident queen. Part of that is also shaped by what *I* was looking for. Since I had *just* started doing drag, I was especially reflexive about my relationship to femininity. Without this attentiveness, I might not have been attuned to the arresting glimpses of femininity that peppered the dance floor. My interlocutors might not have divulged to me their complex relationships with femininity. In fact, when I attend queer desi parties now, I am overwhelmed by the hypermasculinity performed in those spaces. Without LaWhore and the ethos she cultivated in and around me, there's the possibility that masculinity might have been the central point of investigation in my study, that I would have ignored the flashes of femme fabulosity and focused only on dominant gender performances.

Ethnographic disciplines obsessively reckon with the role of the researcher, and rightly so. This is a research method that is deeply implicated in the management of colonial subjects, in constructing knowledge about racial others that directly or inadvertently justifies their subjugation. Precisely because of this pattern of exploitation, both historical and ongoing, ethnography must take seriously who the researcher is and what they do in the field. Drag insists that knowledge is not neutral. It calls on me to account for *how* I know what I know in the field.

Knowing that I am *in drag* in the field, whether as LaWhore the queen or as Kareem the researcher, makes concrete the way my body and being are impacting the content of my research. LaWhore and Kareem elicit different data and elicit data differently. Having LaWhore reminds me that Kareem too is a persona. From the illegibility of my ethnicity and caste as a diasporic Sindhi *bhaiband* in South India, to my Muslim first name, to my beard, to my drag—everything about me shapes who does and doesn't want to talk to me in the field and about what. Performing as LaWhore has certainly made me a safer subject for women, trans men, and nonbinary folks to interact with—at the club, and after. LaWhore, gaudy and girly and visibly queer, has also made some masculine men who ventured to Chicago from the suburbs seeking a discreet place to party, turn on their heels and leave *Jai Ho!* immediately. Drag queens? Ew!

LaWhore's work taught me to navigate space and time differently. I had to relearn what a nightclub was: arriving *before* the doors opened to see the space in its dusty nakedness under garish fluorescent lighting, getting ready in the basement among financial ledgers and old event posters. I also learned a new material geography of the cities I lived in by shopping for clothes and accessories at stores that other drag queens told me about. I'd venture to wholesale fashion warehouses—So Good in Chicago's Uptown or Earrings Plaza in NYC's Midtown—in search of cheap jewelry. I would witness the bling affinities, the sweetly strange intimacies of white drag queens asking Arab and Nigerian aunties, "Do these earrings look good on me?" Shopping to dress LaWhore gave *me* the impetus to walk down aisles of the thrift store that I had never explored and a reason to enter fashion boutiques that I never gave myself permission to visit. Shopping to dress LaWhore gave me permission to be gayer. If you've met me, you may wonder how that's possible. But LaWhore works miracles!

> **Drag insists that knowledge is not neutral, calling on me to account for *how* I know what I know.**

Access to cheap bling spurred me to buy rhinestoned necklaces and pendants for myself. Not just masculine Cuban links, but cutesy Hello Kitty figures, fruits, and farm animals. These accessories became my signature for a few years. Adding that affordable shine to my body, whether in or out of drag, invited attention in the nightclub. One night, at a party in Bangalore, someone stopped me as I wandered around the edge of the dance floor. He placed his hand on my chest, on the giant rhinestoned heart-shaped pendant I was wearing, "I like it," he said. "You're always wearing some interesting necklace." Dhaval and I became friendly at the parties I attended and he agreed to an interview. As we talked, he told me the story of being possessed by the spirit of actress Sridevi after watching her snake dance in the film *Nagina*. This story became central to *Ishtyle*, to understanding the relationship between screen divas and queer dancers. Had LaWhore not needed bling, Kareem might not have had that interview, and I might not have dived deep into the world of diva worship.

FIELDWORK DIVA

My reputation as a drag queen in Chicago opened doors for me in Bangalore. Drag not only prescribed my research agenda in Bangalore to center feminine aesthetics, but it led me to the figure of the diva. By thinking with how divas haunt the dance floor, I was obligated to think about women's labor in primarily men's spaces.

I entered Bangalore's queer nightlife scene through Mithun, a friend LaWhore made on the dance floor of *Jai Ho!* in Chicago. He grasped LaWhore's shoulder-padded shoulders when "Aaja Nachle" came on the speakers: "I love this song!" "Aaja Nachle" (Come and dance) is the title song of Madhuri Dixit's comeback to the blockbuster screen, and it is not insignificant that Madhuri brought Mithun and me together. Mithun had to return to India, having recently been laid off from his IT job following the 2008 economic downturn. This was precisely the time I started traveling to Bangalore for research. Thanks to Mithun, my reputation as a drag queen preceded me across the pond, where I was invited to choreograph for friends and for strangers, providing an inbuilt way to learn about their dance, bodies, and histories.

In anticipation of a queer cultural festival, friends asked if I would perform: "You do drag, right? You should choreograph for us!" Like my friends in Chicago who asked what LaWhore would perform at the next *Jai Ho!*, people in Bangalore requested dance from me. Feeling the obligation to be an obedient ethnographer and do what my interlocutors asked of me, I put up a public Facebook post inviting folks to come to a rehearsal. The Pink Divas were born. We didn't intentionally name ourselves, but one of the songs in that first medley we performed was the Kannada hit "Padmavati" that begins with "Deevah Deevah!" One day, my friend Seshadri referred to us as the Pink Divas, and that was it. The name stuck.

Dancing with the Pink Divas opened up *other* ways of getting to know my interlocutors beyond what the nightclub afforded. My interviews with the Pink Divas were especially rich because of the intimacy we cultivated sweating and eating and dancing together. When I asked these friends how they started dancing and why they loved dance, many answered that Indian actresses Sridevi and Madhuri Dixit were integral to sparking their obsessions. It took me by surprise how standardized these answers were, almost always following the same outline. Like Dhaval, the Pink Divas told me that Sridevi and Madhuri functioned as a conduit toward transcendence,

My interviews with the Pink Divas were especially rich because of the intimacy we cultivated sweating and eating and dancing together.

something more than. They talked about how some family members encouraged reenactments of these transgressive dances. They also described being reprimanded by family members for these dangerous choreographies.

I had heard these songs growing up, but Madhuri and Sridevi weren't *my* divas. In fact, I didn't have my own diva! See, there *was* room to be more gay! The subject of diva worship is a well-worn story in queer studies, from the early twentieth-century fandoms of prima ballerinas and opera singers to lesbian desires in the musical theatre hall, from Mexican Americans' devotion to Selena Quintanilla to Lady Gaga and Katy Perry's neoliberal co-opting of diva worship by pandering to gay audiences. But divas were not on my research agenda until my interlocutors asked me to think critically about them.

When writing a research proposal, you're expected to name the interpretive tools you plan to use in order to approach your archive or field site. But then there are the analytical tools we encounter and start to employ *while* doing primary research. Spending time with the Pink Divas was its own methods class, providing new tools for analysis as I acclimatized to the interpretive lens with which they experienced the world. Their insistence on the empowering nature of femininity, alongside their choreographies that accessed freedom and play through the screen, led me to ask new questions about nightlife. My interlocutors prompted me to look more closely at the relationship between media and materiality, diva and dance floor, film and fandom. This, to me, is the most exciting part of ethnography: to let field research lead you rather than arrive knowing what you want to find. Proposals and prospectuses certainly offer structure, and are helpful templates to return to when you feel a bit lost at sea while doing research. But *Ishtyle* is built around the unexpected, around those moments in which my research revealed to me that which I could not have anticipated.

I dedicate a chapter in *Ishtyle* to two Bollywood divas, Madhuri and Sridevi. I document how their diva gestures appear in the club, follow their personal histories on and off screen, and read these performances *through* my interlocutors' interviews. This interdisciplinary method allows me to explore dance's capacity to engage with one's past selves on the dance floor, as well as its ability to conjure new embodiments and desires in the club.

Listening to diva narratives from my friends also led LaWhore to perform Madhuri and Sridevi songs at *Jai Ho!*, which then incited responses from other interlocutors. "That song was a garba favorite." "The last time I heard that song was when sitting on my grandmother's lap." "That's *my* song." Drag became a laboratory to test out how widespread this diva worship ran. Putting divas on my body incited further diva discourse. Performance is not only a way of gathering data; it's a way of interpreting it too. In the show "Cuir Devotion," drag queen Penelope Sumac lip-synchs the words of interlocutors in scholar Enzo Toral's research. Toral, who studies Andean queer and trans Indigenous performance, lip-synchs his interlocutors' words in order to get closer to the dynamic textuality and aurality of their speech. Knowledge lies not only in what people say but in how they say it. Penelope offers a way, a reason, to embody these voices. In so doing, she makes more sense of the research data. Much like LaWhore's performances of the iconic Sridevi and Madhuri numbers I learned about in my interviews, Toral/Sumac's drag becomes a way of mining data for more meaning.

Lip-synch is also a way of staging *both* one's proximity to and difference from an other. Summer Kim Lee writes beautifully about how lip-synch teaches the performer to become a student of the other. As a student of an other's voice or dance, you learn both about the quotidian virtuosity they embody, and the limits of your own body to approximate theirs. Margot Weiss reveals how researchers are usually the ones credited as expert theorists offering something new to the world through their interpretation of what interlocutors say. To me, lip-synch offers an instructive tool to confer ex-

Lip-synch is also a way of staging *both* one's proximity to and difference from an other.

pertise and artistry on the interlocutor, while simultaneously revealing the scholar's interpretive work.

I performed Madhuri and Sridevi's diva femininity according to what I'd experienced in the field. But there were reactions to my staging that gathered *more* ideas about what these divas mean, how they circulate, and why they matter. In a similar vein, the volunteer work I did with Bengaluru Pride when I was in India for my fieldwork made me realize quite quickly that I could not simply be a participant observer. I was expected to curate, perform, to be a diva, a certain *kind* of gay. As a drag queen from the US, there was an expectation that I brought with me a fabulous emancipatory individualism.

I progressively became aware of how I was being situated by my interlocutors, even amidst my fellow Pink Divas. The kinds of cultural capital I brought with me: short shorts and blingy necklaces. I was gayly fabulous for wearing short shorts to organizing meetings, and also an immodest NRI for thinking I could wear them to the police station to file for permission to hold the festival. "You stay in the car. We'll go in." Through questions, offhand comments, and jokes, I became aware of the underlying interest people had in affiliating with me, specifically knowledge I could offer about visa processing and US hiring practices. Given my regular travel between the US and India, someone even asked me to launder money for his family business.

I slowly learned the cultural knowledge we were supposed to share as desi queers: "Choli ke Peeche," "Hawa Hawai," Madhuri, Sridevi. My fellow dancers tested and evaluated my diva knowledge. When Hari was teaching a step for his section of our dance medley, he described it as "like Madhuri's, from *Sailaab*." My blank stare suggesting I had no idea what he was talking about made him scowl in judgment. Had I not invested in a diva yet? Had I not repeatedly watched and rehearsed Madhuri's dances? His scowl questioned the Indianness of my queerness, my commitment to a certain kind of beauty and femininity, my investment in an archive and repertoire of Indian grace made and modeled by Madhuri Dixit.

The way Hari tested my knowledge was just one example of how my interlocutors had expectations of me. They required me to enter the logics of their everyday life, while also asking questions of my own. Not knowing how Madhuri moved in *Sailaab* was significant. Hari's reaction gave me a sliver of information about what was important to him, but also reminded me that I had an obligation to catch up to the way he and the other Pink Divas made value out of popular culture. However empiricist I might have wanted to be, there was no room for objectivity or detachment. I was required to cultivate a different common sense.

In teaching me about divas, on and off screen, the Pink Divas made a media studies scholar out of me.

In teaching me about divas, on and off screen, the Pink Divas made a media studies scholar out of me. Scholarship on divas, particularly that of Lauren Berlant and Deborah Paredez, has taught me how to care for divas when I perform them in drag: Whitney, Céline, Iqbal Bano, Sridevi, Madhuri, Nicki Minaj, Helen, Celia Cruz, Gloria Gaynor, Usha Uthup. These are all women whose health, bodies, morality, accent, grammar, sexuality, voice, and dress have been scrutinized in the public sphere even as they generously gifted us the aesthetic tools to survive cisheteropatriarchy. To perform them requires knowing their story, taking good care of their dignity and virtuosity. My interlocutors in Bangalore not only taught me the value of diva worship, but led me to diva scholarship, which has in turn shaped my drag practice.

The urgency of the diva left me thinking, "How have I gotten this far in life *without* divas?" And then I remembered my aunties.

AUNTYLECTUAL

My current book-in-progress, *Auntologies: Queer Aesthetics and South Asian Aunties*, explores the aunty as a significant figure through which critical social commentaries are staged in South Asian diasporic public cultures. I arrived at this project *through* drag.

As I wrote about and theorized the stories my friends told me about being disciplined into certain kinds of gender performances by their family when they danced like Sridevi and Madhuri as kids, I had to reflect on my own histories of gendering. Where had I learned the aspirational paradigms of femininity that made me feel like an imposter in drag, with my inexpensive polyester saris and hairy forearms? My aunties. My interlocutors described rewinding and rewatching VHS tapes of Hindi films to study diva gestures. I too repeatedly watched videos of my mother and aunties performing at Diwali shows and other nighttime functions in Ghana. These videos, recording the brief amateur skits and dances that my aunties rehearsed as the gala's entertainment, taught me the feminine choreographies that my aunties themselves would not.

These aunty choreographies function as an origin story to my own drag practice. My aunties regularly performed in masculine drag for these infrequent shows: tucking long hair underneath the collar of button-down shirts to become Amitabh Bachchan and sketching mustaches on their cleanly waxed upper lips to transform into Raj Kapoor. They'd rehearse in our living room, their masculine-feminine flirtations on display with no men gazing at them, just my proto-gay eyes peering up from my chemistry textbooks, inscribing the choreography into my brain.

My aunties regularly performed in masculine drag: tucking long hair underneath the collar of button-down shirts to become Amitabh Bachchan and sketching mustaches on their cleanly waxed upper lips to transform into Raj Kapoor.

I like to route my drag narrative through my aunties. LaWhore primarily performs Bollywood numbers, but white men regularly tell her she is "so good at camp." My overexaggerated gestures, facial expressions, and demure eye contact can be read through an Old Hollywood episteme. Beginning my diva narrative with my aunties offers a different aesthetic lens through which to interpret my exaggerated embodiment: still camp but of a different genealogy.

My aunties were the conduits between me and Bollywood divas because, living in Ghana in the 1980s and '90s, we didn't have easy access to Hindi film VHSs. When a new movie arrived in town in the suitcase of someone who had just come back from India or Dubai, the VHS was passed around from home to home to watch. There were anxious phone calls between aunties: "Have you watched it yet? I can watch it tonight and send it back to you tomorrow morning." My aunties cobbled together choreography from this circulating video archive, and I then mimicked their amateur dances without having ever seen the films that inspired them. Truly, there are scores of dances I've done for which I'm only seeing the original choreography *now* that older film song-and-dance sequences have been uploaded to YouTube by big production houses.

I wrote about how my aunties shaped LaWhore's choreographies in an essay titled "Aunty Fever: A Queer Impression." But something about the "Aunty Fever" essay felt apocryphal. Those childhood memories felt unreliable. Although I trusted my interlocutors' stories of proto-queer childhood performance, my own drag origins felt more fallible. Academic empiricism, and the supposed objectivity it calls for, made me question my own memory.

In 2019, I made a research trip to archives in Ghana to see as many community performance videos as I could from the 1980s and 1990s. When I rewatched those videos, not only did I meet many aunties in masculine drag, I also encountered some uncles in feminine drag too! I was glad to know my drag king aunties were real. But it was also so clear why I hadn't retained memories of drag queen uncles as proto-queer possibilities. The men did drag in ways that undermined femininity, putting it on in order to laugh at it, doing it lazily. However, the women staged masculinity earnestly, expertly, and with effort. They therefore looked sexy and confident doing so. They enjoyed it. No wonder they left a queer impression. I admit to being a rabid scholar of performance, insisting on the value of the embodied, remembered, ephemeral. But there was something very satisfying about seeing "the archive" and being assured that my wild memories of aunty drag kings were not simply figments of my imagination.

When I presented "Aunty Fever" at the Association for Asian American Studies conference one year, a South Asian audience member stood up to say, "I can see what you're trying to do in this essay, but I just can't get behind it. And maybe it's because I'm a woman. And the ways that aunties have constantly disciplined me and been wicked to me." This moment lives in my memory as one of those primal scenes in which another academic "came for me." I was embarrassed and defensive and I lost trust in my intellectual compass. But when those feelings dissipated, I was able to return to that moment to ask where the commenter and I converged and diverged.

It slowly became clear to me that when I use "aunty" to refer to the women who raised me, I am hailing the many feelings, aesthetics, and moral ecologies discursively attached to the term "aunty" itself. It is a highly charged term. Aunties, those women and femme figures who orbit the nuclear family, are often thought of as surveilling young people's gender, sexuality, and morality. For this reason, young people often depict aunties as having excessive, monstrous genders. Aunties scrutinize young people, young people demonize aunties; this loops as a vicious cycle that occludes other acts of care within and across generations.

The term "aunty" is so stigmatized that "Don't call me aunty" is its own meme. TikTok, YouTube, and Instagram content featuring some kind of "Don't call me aunty" refrain is endless; these memes motivated me to ask how "aunty" becomes such a loaded term. To begin exploring this question, I've been amassing an archive of aunty objects: board

When I refer to the women who raised me as "aunty," I am hailing the many feelings, aesthetics, and moral ecologies discursively attached to "aunty," a highly charged term.

games, tote bags, t-shirts, memes, media, artworks, literature, and more. Also, while I slowly build the aunty book project, I've edited two special journal issues on aunties that have helped me understand the aunty as an abundant figure for social critique. She is—we are—a fulcrum around which to theorize age, disability, fatness, kinship, colonial history, architecture, desire, geography, temporality, and more. As a queer studies scholar thinking about aunties, I want to expand on aunty sexualities and sexy aunties. Aunties are regularly stereotyped as foreclosing queer futures for young people, and I've written against this narrative to imagine the queer futures aunties build between themselves.

What is at stake in narrating aunties otherwise? Like that commenter at the conference, I too have aunties who fat-shamed me, questioned my masculinity, and commented on my dark skin and unmarriageability. But I worry that focusing on aunties only as moralizing agents of the state—panopticaunts if you will—stigmatizes their aesthetic practices as well. Aunties, bursting in and out of the living room, invited or not, expand the aesthetic world of the home, creating more opportunities for fantasy and self-fashioning by infiltrating the limits of the nuclear family. As LaWhore Vagistan says, "My aunties taught me that leopard print is a neutral. And that sequins are daywear." My aunties inspired my love of bling, saris, dance, storytelling, drama, hospitality, and gossip.

As LaWhore says, "My aunties taught me that leopard print is a neutral. And that sequins are daywear."

Aunties are very much originators of my drag. But the truth is that my aunties offered me aesthetics, but didn't intentionally gift them to me. They didn't teach me how to drape, pleat, or pin a sari; this wasn't the proper knowledge for boys. I had to study these practices surreptitiously. My drag beginnings in Chicago relied on ephemeral acts of kindness: a partygoer insisting he retie my sari at the club, a roommate teaching me how to put a bra on back to front first, a friend's partner taking me to Sally's Beauty to buy my first makeup. In her early days, LaWhore had very little sustained mentorship as she experimented with femininity.

Some friends say they miss early LaWhore and her edgy, genderfuck style. But back then, I skipped wigs because I couldn't afford them. And because I didn't know how to style or pin them. My makeup was unruly because I didn't know how to contour; I didn't grasp the sculptural work contouring was supposed to do on the face. I didn't wear pads because I didn't fully understand that feminine clothes were cut to fit curves I did not have. Control over my image came six years into my drag career, with *Drag Class*.

Drag Class was a ten-week competition I took part in at a nightclub in Austin in 2016, that involved lessons, homework, and grades as a means of supporting participants in growing their drag practice. The final challenge of *Drag Class* was to perform a song parody, and I wrote "Sari" to the tune of Justin Bieber's "Sorry."

Yo yo, we are live debuting LaWhore Vagistan's first-ever single!

I don't want to look like all of the other drag queens
Leggings for days, dresses for miles, and gowns for weeks
Chanel and Dior, Louis Vuitton, Versace
'Cuz I look best, when I'm dressed like an aunty.

Don't I look great in this sari?
'Cuz I'm giving you this sexy body.
Don't I look great in this sari?
I know right now I look so fly, when I rock my desi style!

That is looking like a 100-rupee sari!
This is such a last-season sari!
Learn to walk properly in that sari!
I know right now I look so fly, when I rock my desi style!

They tell me I'm hairy, should invest in some Nair but I say no.
"Your skin is too dark and you need a highlight and more contour."
You know what? I'll own it, won't be mad when you call me "curry-scented ho."
'Cuz I'm not stressed, hashtag blessed, namaslay bitch!

Don't I look great in this sari?
'Cuz I'm giving you this sexy body
Don't I look great in this sari?
I know right now I look so fly, when I rock my desi style!

You don't wanna mess with this aunty
'Cuz she'll put that salt in your chai tea.
Don't I look great in this sari?
I know right now I look so fly, when I rock my desi style!

The pleats are uneven on your sari!
You need to nicely pin your sari!
Where can I also buy that sari?
I know right now I look so fly, when I rock my desi style!

You look like Priyanka Chopra in that sari!
You'll find your life partner in that sari!
You look rocking in that sari!
I know right now I look so fly, when I rock my desi style!

This is Aunty Kool Jamz with LaWhore Vagistan.
Chalo, we're out.
Time to sip some chai and play that rummy.
Peace out *betas*!

Though I sang the song live at the competition finale, it was in the recording studio that the track emerged as one *about* aunties. I invited my friend and collaborator Vyjayanthi "Aunty Kool Jamz" Vadrevu to help lay down the track. The hope was that her expertly trained sound would flesh out my tentative voice, which needed heavy autotuning. She was supposed to sing the chorus only. However, our music producer suggested she record spoken fillers during instrumental interludes. As we sat to brainstorm lines, it became clear that the idea of aunty functioned as a commonsense figure through which we understood our diasporic genders and desires. The lines flowed. "That is looking like a 100-rupee sari," and "This is such a last-season sari." Her arc develops over the course of the song, and she shifts from critical aunty to complimentary aunty—"You look rocking in that sari!"—praising LaWhore for her furry femme fashion. This was an important moment in which "aunty" as a discursive category emerged *between* us; our shared understandings of aunty-ness made it easy to concoct lyrics. Just as performing Madhuri and Sridevi incited *more* diva discourse, performing aunty incited *more* aunty content.

Uploading the "Sari" music video to YouTube quickly shifted LaWhore into the public role of aunty. Here she was with a studio-recorded song, a professionally shot and edited video, new makeup skills she learned in *Drag Class,* styled wigs, sophisticated in her wardrobe of saris. And then of course the lyrics, "I look best when I'm dressed like an aunty," and "You don't wanna mess with this aunty, 'cuz she'll put that salt in your chai tea." She entered the public domain more polished than ever before—no longer the edgy, experimental, messy queen on the makeshift Chicago stage. Now she had a part to play: aunty, a pillar of memory, authority, and beauty.

Circulating this music video transformed LaWhore's public image and made her lean into aunty-ness. But its reception, the uptake of LaWhore as "aunty" by others, raised new research questions. Why did people resonate so swiftly with her as aunty? Why were saris central to conjuring aunty-ness? Why did Vyjayanthi and I have such easy access to ideas of how aunties act and what aunties say? My creative practice has been central to developing research questions, questions that are both close to my own body and life and experiences, and larger, more discursive questions about gender, kinship, aesthetics, bodies, dress, power, and media. Letting drag and research inform each other has not only kept my research agenda alive after the exhaustion of writing the dissertation and first book, it has made research a dynamic and nourishing kind of work.

Letting drag and research inform each other has not only kept my research agenda alive, it has made research a dynamic and nourishing kind of work.

AUNTY ON STAGE

LaWhore not only writes with and about me, she also performs and lectures about my research. In her solo show *Lessons in Drag*, Dr. Vagistan offers a ninety-minute lecture performance in which she explains key ideas from her favorite academic, Dr. Khubchandani, followed by lip synchs inspired by his writing. She concretizes the relationship between performance and research, performing a number about call centers based on my research on Indian accents, and explaining the notion of the model minority through a spelling-bee-themed number. When I speak about my research in third person, as LaWhore, it keeps scholarship alive, on my lips and in my body, rather than relegating it to textual form that I put on the page a decade ago. The show requires me to rehearse the connections between my different scholarly projects as I move from section to section, and to demonstrate how they are routed through LaWhore and through drag.

Performing my research is an act of interpretation in service of further analysis, as I explained above. Additionally, putting research on my body reminds me of the urgency of my own work, of its very material nature. Bodies *hold* politics. My research comes to life in my body. When I perform, I am reminded *why* thinking about accents, aunties, and affect matters. When I lip-synch as the diasporic Indian child competing in a spelling bee, —"May I have the language of origin please?"—I feel the tightness, obedience, and restraint that model minority myths bind to the body. When I perform the call center worker graduating into a new identity—"I'm Shilpi Gupta, and my new call center name is Carol Lopez! Thank you!"—I have to reckon with the joy and excitement for the future in her voice despite my critique of global labor structures. When I lip-synch Hindi and Spanish translations of "I Will Survive" as part of the "Critical Aunty Studies" section of the show, I experience the song *beyond* textual replication. Instead, each of the three versions become rhythmic and emotional reinventions that speak *with* each other rather than mimic any one authoritative original.

Bodies *hold* politics. My research comes to life in my body. When I perform, I am reminded *why* thinking about accents, aunties, and affect matters.

Drag is a potent venue through which to stage critical research. Canadian Indo-Caribbean queen Tifa Wine uses photography and film to stage Ryan Persadie's research on indenture, feminism, and mythology. Persadie's research on the uses of festive performance in queer, post-indenture diasporas is consolidated in Tifa's annual Coolie-ween photo series. In these portraits and a subsequent film, Tifa stages the ghostly and monstrous figures emerging from the violence of patriarchy, colonialism, and indenture that Persadie has learned about in his research. Drag becomes a repository to hold research, to make sense of critical findings, to put them on the body, into the public sphere, and invigorate them with flesh.

The show *Lessons in Drag* operates as a guided tour of my publications, from my work on nightlife and drag, to my exploration of race and religion, to my new writing about aunties. More than once, colleagues have made the joke, "That was a great job talk!" It's both a silly and cynical comment. It mocks the gaucheness of exhibiting my own research so lavishly. Certainly, LaWhore says things about me like, "Wow, he's written about *everything*!" and "Isn't he brilliant?" I won't apologize for being cringe. But there is *another* level of research LaWhore is doing that I think non-academics see and appreciate in the performance. Her performances are supposed to complement my research, but they also exceed my scholarship as their own *kind* of research as well.

LaWhore's performances are supposed to complement my research, but they also exceed my scholarship as their own *kind* of research.

The performance numbers in *Lessons in Drag* are the result of rigorous research in themselves. They involve searching for and arranging archives; coding video and sound clips to find the relationship between them; assembling sound, gesture, image, and costume in ways that communicate a set of ideas to the audience. Sure, it is my scholarship and that of my academic interlocutors that LaWhore draws on to stage structural Islamophobia or the pressures of assimilation. But for the purposes of a performance, I have to put together sound- and image-scapes that can actually stage these ideas. These are not the objects I analyze in my publications. I have endured hours of interviews, documentaries, podcasts, newscasts about call centers, spelling bees, racial profiling just to find the right sound bites. I've listened to every version of "I Will Survive," "A Whole New World," and "Damadam Mast Qalandar," as well as every song by Fergie. I grew delirious, and furious, watching footage of the British Royal family in search of clips. This is the weird shit you do when putting together a drag number: You do research. You disappear for hours and days into

Drag artists are phenomenal researchers, excavating visual, material, choreographic, and sartorial archives to collage their performances.

thrift stores, Pinterest pages, YouTube, Instagram, Soundcloud, Spotify, Google Images. Drag artists are phenomenal researchers. They excavate visual, material, choreographic, and sartorial archives to collage their performances. Making a drag number is its own kind of critical synthesis, its own kind of essaying.

When I stage my research in drag, I am also staging drag *as* research, and I'm hoping that the show offers a model for others to see drag as a critical intellectual practice. Because I primarily perform on college campuses, I often hear people say, "This was my first live drag show!" It makes sense. Live drag in the US primarily appears in twenty-one-and-older spaces so even out queer and trans students have only had access to drag on screens. Drag newbies will often comment, "I didn't know drag could be so 'smart'"—to which LaWhore replies that even though she's citing scholarly research, the *form* of what she does looks very much like drag in nightclubs. Drag *is* smart; it is analytical; it can tell a story; and it can make an argument.

UNBECOMING TO ACADEMIA

I'm not sure who I thought I would become after grad school, although at one point I foresaw the elbow-patched, gray haired, pipe-smoking daddy as my future. Come to think of it, there was at least one tweed blazer with suede elbow patches in my graduate closet. I felt *very* cool wearing it with mismatched Converse. "I'm not like the other professors. I'm a cool professor." Now I'm wearing saris to teach, writing essays about aunties having sex, giving students feedback like "Try it more slutty next time!" This future could not have been foretold.

I'm left thinking about what is possible when we let research transform us, when we track what becomes of us in the process of doing research. What happens to our research agendas as we too are moved by our studies? For me, research has offered bodily autonomy, pleasure, and art. It has made me gayer, more beautiful, more politically engaged, sillier. It has given me fashion, dance, and community. What has *your* research made of you?

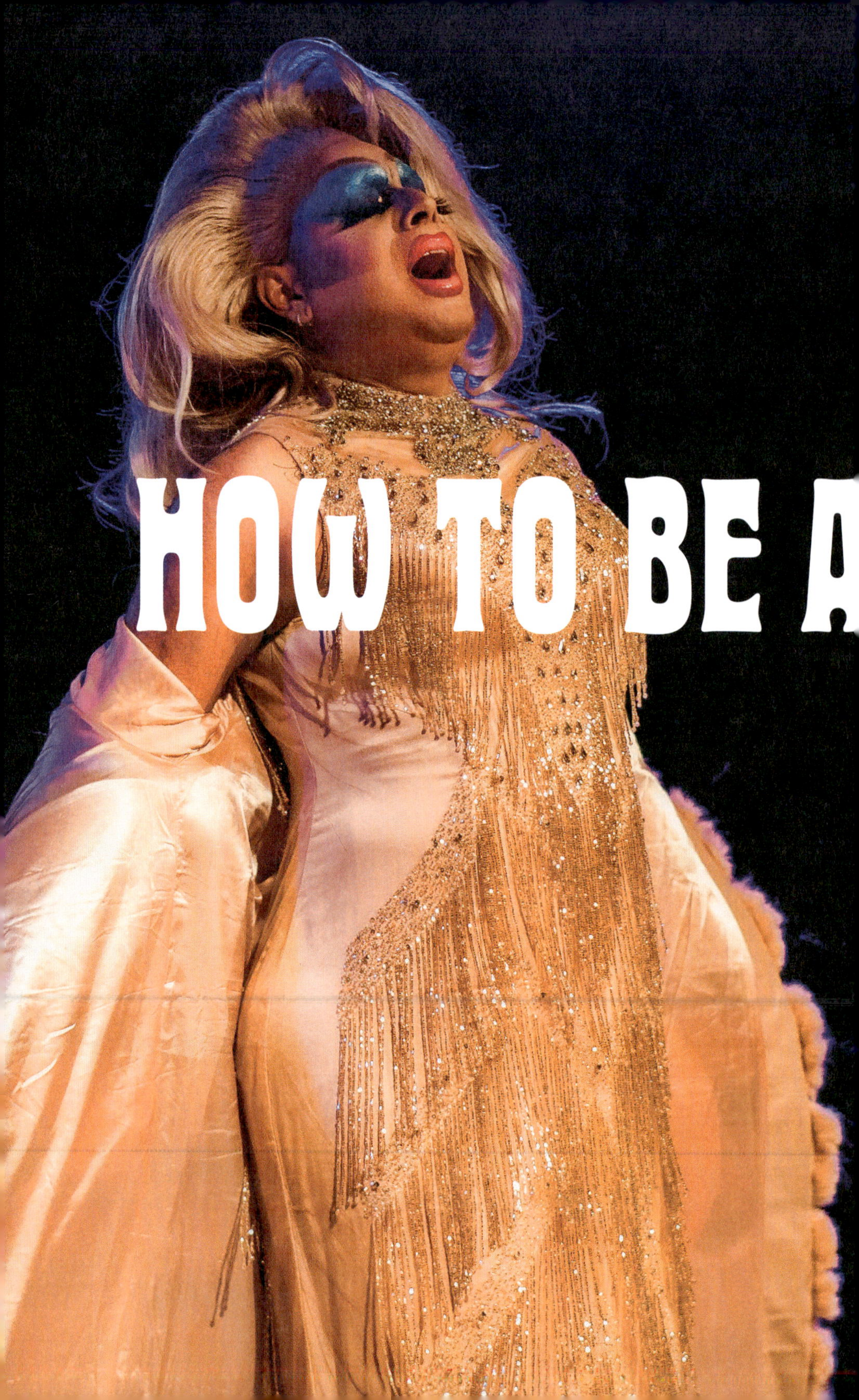

HOW TO BE A

DRAG QUEEN

Hi LaWhore. I hope you're well.
I emailed you my first chapter
a few weeks ago.Hope you received it.

Rcvd.

Was wondering what you thought?

Hv not read yet.

Oh ok, will you let me
know when you have?

Hi LaWhore. Was wondering
if you'd read the chapter?

omg. Hi dear. Frgt to msg
yes, read. V good. A bit lpng.
will write this week.
But nt sure where 2 start.

What about
at the very beginning?
Your first show?

OK. And then?

Just see where it takes you?

OK. Will try. 💋

MY FIRST TIME

I'm back! Thought you'd never hear from me again after all that long-winded meandering from Dr. Khubchandani?! Come, lay your head in Aunty's bosoms and let me tell you a story. Let me take you to a distant and fantastic land called Chicago! We'll go faaaaaaar back in time to the early twenty-first century.

It was the summer of 2009. Bollywood fever was in the air. *Slumdog Millionaire* took home four Golden Globes, seven BAFTAs, and eight Oscars. The Academy Award for best original song? "Jai Ho!" by A. R. Rahman and Gulzar. The song was playing in every bar in the city, and it was wild to see Rahman's face on the screens of gay bars like Sidetrack and Roscoe's! Naturally, we decided to call our queer desi party *Jai Ho!* By we, I mean members of Trikone-Chicago—a fledgling organization for queer South Asian community and activism. There were many other names we could have landed on that would have invoked something sexier or more nostalgic. But we went with *Jai Ho!* because we needed the white people to understand that we meant "Bollywood." We needed white money—this was a fundraiser after all!

Dev Patel was sexy, and the gays were thirsty for "Bollywood." But the appetite for drag was large too! The first season of *RuPaul's Drag Race* had just aired on Logo TV. With frontrunners like Nina Flowers, BeBe Zahara Benet, and Ongina in that season, diasporic drag was having a moment, and it felt necessary to feature drag at *Jai Ho!* Drag has long been part of queer South Asian party spaces. *Club Kali*, a party in London that began in 1995, not only routinely books drag queens, but many partygoers beeline straight for the bathroom to change into their alter egos and revel in a new dress for the night on the dance floor. Iconic queens like Bijli would make pop-up appearances at *Desilicious* in New York City in the early 2000s. And Queen Harish came all the way from India to perform at parties in San Francisco and New York in 2008. So, *Drag Race* wasn't the only reason drag felt important to *Jai Ho!* A queer desi night just wasn't a queer desi night without drag. But where to find a drag queen?

Enter me! LaWhore Vagistan! I was barely a drag anything then. Dr. Khubchandani's thesis show was my first appearance, for all of twenty-five minutes. But as my new friends in Trikone and I tried to locate South Asian drag artists to perform for *Jai Ho!* we couldn't find any. There were people who cross-dressed at house parties. There were trans women who did filmi *mujras*, but only in the privacy of domestic spaces where their transfemininity was celebrated and adored. But I couldn't locate any "professionals" who would perform in public.

So I went shopping. A long bob from the Chinese beauty store beside my apartment. Weak foundations and powdery eyeshadows from Sally's Beauty. A sequin top and flared skirt from the Salvation Army on Devon—the Indo-Pak neighborhood. More sequins from the Dollar Store to decorate the skirt. Voilà. Drag! I used Audacity to mix "Chamma Chamma" (a song I was sure the white gays would know because of *Moulin Rouge*) and "Paper Planes" (a song I knew the white gays would know because of MIA). It's wild to me how much I kept white audiences in mind back then—but, like I said, we needed their money. And, anyway, "Chamma Chamma" is an iconic Bollywood item song in its own right. Remember Urmila vigorously pulsing her chest and jingling all that silver jewelry? "Paper Planes" was very much a diaspora anthem, the (long gone) moment when MIA promised to be the voice denouncing fascism and border surveillance in pop music. So sure, my song choices pandered to white gays. But they were also a gift to my fellow brown queers. I'm kind of a renaissance woman that way.

That first show was a blur: the exhilaration and adrenaline of performing solo for the first time in a nightclub, for a sea of strangers singing along to your lip synch, twirling in garments you've never worn, and trying to tame a shake-and-go wig that un-consensually wants to enter your mouth. I wouldn't have remembered any of it if my friend Zach Blair had not recorded it all for *his* dissertation fieldwork. My favorite moment in his video is when I lose balance and fall off the stage—technically a foot-wide bench running along the side of the bar—and the crowd catches me by the shoulders and pushes me back. And I just keep dancing! Oh, to be twenty-six again!

But also, twenty-six! What internalized homophobia and transphobia allowed Dr. Khubchandani to say he wanted to research drag queens, but had never thought about doing it himself? What internalized homophobia and transphobia allowed Dr. Khubchandani to say he wanted to research drag queens, but had never thought about doing it himself? He must have *really* wanted the attention of the American Eagle–wearing masc4mascs. How else can you explain the fact that, as much as he loved the artform, he had never dreamt of giving it a try until then?

What internalized homophobia and transphobia allowed Dr. Khubchandani to say he wanted to research drag queens, but had never thought about doing it himself?

Anyways, that was it. My debut—and also my swan song. This was all meant to be a one-time thing. But other queer party organizers were dazzled by the novelty of desi drag and invited me to perform at their events. And then, *Jai Ho!* happened again, and again, and so I kept performing. Fifteen years later, *Jai Ho!* continues to run with my drag sibling Masala Sapphire at the helm. Since then, I have toured my solo show *Lessons in Drag*, been photographed for the *New York Times*, *Vogue India*, and *Paper Magazine*, won a drag competition in Austin, given a TEDx talk, made several music videos, taught university classes about drag, and conducted workshops on how to actually do it. I think it's fair to say: I've arrived; I am the expert; and I have a lot to tell you.

So let's talk about it. How do *you* become a drag queen?

NAME! THAT! QUEEN!

First off you need a drag name. With a drag name, you tell an audience who you are even before they meet you. "Sharon Needles" tells them you're a little bit dangerous; "Manila Luzon" tells them you're very Filipina; "Miz Cracker" tells them you don't take yourself so seriously (although unfortunately, she did! Poor thing!). With a drag name you call into presence the communities you feel closest to. Names like "Faluda Islam," "RuAfza," or "Kulfi Jaan" sniff out the South Asian audience through nostalgia, food, and drink. "Jasmine Rice," "Miss Shu Mai," "Bibingka Mama" also use food to summon other Asian communities. "Vaginal Davis," "Harriet Tugsman," "King Molasses," "Lena Horné" summon Black histories of plantation labor, fugitivity, radical activism, and creative protest. Names like these not only politicize their Blackness, they insist on the important of sexuality. A name can invoke a sensation, like "Sasha Velour": soft, velvety, and iridescent. Or nature's glamour: "Pearl," "Amethyst," "Sapphira." Or high art: "Untitled Queen." Or pop culture: "Marcia Marcia Marcia." Your name is a powerful tool to

> **With a drag name, you tell an audience who you are even before they meet you. Your name is a powerful tool to locate yourself for the audience, to give them a taste of whom to expect, even if you end up defying those very expectations.**

locate yourself for the audience, to give them a taste of whom to expect, even if you end up defying those very expectations. My drag name gives me something to come back to when I get too mired in the "who am I?" of it all.

My name is LaWhore Vagistan. Lahore like the city in Pakistan. And like the city, I too am old, cosmopolitan, and have had *many* merchants come through me. Lahore, but with a W, because . . . I'm here to work. And because sex work is real work. And Vagistan, like Pakistan, Hindustan, Afghanistan, Uzbekistan, Bangladeshistan, Sri Lankistan, Nepalistan, Burmistan . . . Your name is a powerful tool to locate yourself for the audience, to give them a taste of whom to expect, even if you end up defying those very expectations. It's a much more expansive vision of the subcontinent, no?

I say this out loud at the top of every show, and it reminds me of the things that I prioritize: geography, violence, sexuality, history, labor. And puns—I love puns! If you read critical scholarship—postcolonial studies and all that—researchers explain the sexualization of the South Asian feminine body, the dressing of the subcontinent as a woman or goddess, the arbitrary nature of lines drawn across the map. My name, LaWhore Vagistan, allows me to embody a different history of gender and sexuality than what was prescribed by colonialism and displacement. And for those who don't read all of that in my name, they hear the word "whore," and decide that they love or hate me based on their biases around sex and sex work. That also does the trick!

EXPOSE YOURSELF!

In order to do drag, you need to see drag! I felt prepared to do drag because I had watched so many other drag artists. I was in awe of the queens at Heaven in New York City, the only eighteen-and-over bar I could find in my college years. They would take over the mic at midnight and make dirty jokes that assured us that sexuality was about joy instead of shame. I took their advice, hence the "whore" part! I would use my brother's ID to attend Shequida's *Gayly Show* at Barracuda every Tuesday night during college summers in New York. I was in awe of her ability to summarize the news, banter with the DJ, flirt with the audience, lip-synch immaculately, and hit operatic high notes every week. If you haven't seen her perform, go today! Go now! Before she croaks! South Asian drag was possible for me because of the queens at *Desilicious*, who transformed Bollywood item girls on the screen into fleshy, sexy, bedazzled starlets mere feet from my own body. I knew the joys of gender play from my aunties, who rehearsed skits and dances for each other in our living room, playing men's *and* women's roles, trading costumes and choreographies to bring *filmi* fantasies to life for each other.

I am a better drag queen *because* I watch drag. I have a sense of how to manage space, time, costume, and audience because I see what works for different audiences. I know how to pace and curate a night, how to carry myself at a solo or group gig, because I've experienced so many different formats. Maybe I shouldn't admit this so freely, but I prefer being in the audience for a show than being in the show myself. Gasp! Listen, this doesn't mean I don't love doing drag. I just love watching drag *that much more*. Feeling FOMO and wonder at the same time fuels my desire to return to the stage gayer and gaudier each time.

I am a better drag queen *because* I watch drag. I have a sense of how to manage space, time, costume, and audience because I see what works for different audiences. I know how to pace and curate a night.

You've probably heard at drag shows, "Support local drag!" Because *Drag Race* trains us to see the show and its stars as the only drag worth paying for, "Support local drag!" is meant to restore attention to the artists who surround you, wherever you live. Yes. Good. Absolutely do that! But also go support foreign drag, or over-there drag, or whatever the opposite of local is. Whether it's via YouTube and Instagram, or while you're on vacation somewhere, look for drag outside your geographic limits. Despite the globalization of *Drag Race*-style drag, it *will* look and sound and feel different when you look elsewhere. From format and length of show, to audience makeup, to curation of content, to the centrality of emceeing, live singing, and lip-synch. The drag in Manila is not the drag in Torremolinos is not the drag in Cape Town is not the drag in San Juan is not the drag in Jakarta. And trust me, I've seen them all! I've learned and grown so much by watching drag in different languages, genders, locations, and cultural registers.

Even though I've been exposed to so many different drag cultures, it's also been helpful to read up more about them. In YouTube's early years, there was a viral video of a Filipina *bakla* artist performing a zombified Whitney Houston who sang "I will always love you" to her lover from beyond the grave. I remain obseeeeessed with this number! Creepy *and* high camp. Cut to 2023, over twenty years later: I read a fabulous scholarly essay by Thea Quiray Tagle that explains the local Filipinx mythologies behind that performance. It made the act even more intriguing and meaningful! Similarly, while I love Selena drag, I really only knew the Chicana popstar through her 1997 biopic starring Jennifer Lopez. Reading scholarship *about* Selena by Deborah Paredez made me understand *why* re-performing her is so powerful, why it hits so hard.

See, it's important to have lessons *in* drag. Reading drag scholarship expands how I watch drag, but also how I do drag. The biographies of divas alongside research about diva worship, camp, fabulosity, performativity, and impersonation has shaped how I perform the diva on stage. And look, I get it: Scholarship could be written in a way that's more available to audiences. It could be more accessible instead of hiding behind a paywall. Someone please tell Dr. Khubchandani that! But if you can get your hands on them, I do think it's helpful to read histories and scholarly analyses of drag and trans performance beyond our immediate worlds and timeframes. As much as I hate to quote Serena ChaCha: "Pick up a book and go read!" Or, like watch a film or documentary—*Paris Is Burning, Venus Boys, Paper Dolls, Madame X, Call Her Ganda, Showgirls of Pakistan*. There are endless resources to broaden what we know about drag, gender performance, and trans politics. They can create a more expansive library of styles, aspirations, and audiences for our own drag.

WHY WAIT?

I perform much less often than I did in my Chicago and Austin days. Dr. Khubchandani's annoying pursuit of scholarly production means that drag can't dictate my schedule or wallet—the one-body problem no one tells you about in the academy. But early on, I said yes to every opportunity: grad student conferences, punky parties, variety shows, pride celebrations. The beer-drenched carpets of a seedy bar. An Art Deco fountain. A grassy Trans Pride festival. Cramped living rooms. Back patios. The rehearsal rooms of Pritzker Pavilion. I've done it all. The latter was a performance installation that involved lip-synching Céline's "It's All Coming Back to Me Now" on repeat for an hour.

I've been paid nothing. I've been compensated in free access to photos from the event. I've been paid twenty-five dollars and two Jell-O shots. But saying yes to all these opportunities, sometimes creating the opportunities myself, meant I got to experiment with what I liked, to learn what felt good in my body. Each performance was a chance to expand my tool kit, a reason to acquire a new article of clothing for my wardrobe, an adventure to suss out a new audience, an obligation to memorize

> **To do drag, you need to *do* it. Don't burn yourself out. Don't go in debt for a gig. But also, don't wait for the "better" thing.**

a new lip synch. To date, "It's All Coming Back to Me Now" remains in my repertoire because of that 2013 performance.

To do drag, you need to *do* it. Constantly deferring opportunities because you're not "ready" or because they don't offer the exposure or payment you want might mean that your practice doesn't build. Don't burn yourself out. Don't go in debt for a gig. But also, don't wait for the "better" thing.

KNOW YOUR AUDIENCE

I do my best to get to know who I'll be performing for because I get really uncomfortable in spaces where I feel like an outsider. I'm there to do a show *with* my audience, not just *for* them, you know? I was once invited to perform at a memorial celebration for an artist who had passed away. Some years prior, he had seen me at another event, and when he curated this party as part of his end-of-life preparations, he included my name on the list of performers he wanted there. I didn't know him and I didn't know the audience. But I was so flattered to be invited that I said yes immediately.

As soon as I got there, I realized I was on the outside of it all, not just because the audience was mostly straight, but in terms of feelings as well. They had gathered in grief and familiarity, and I was there to do a *show*! Perhaps it was a mistake to open with my Nicki Minaj number. No, it was *definitely* a mistake to open with my Nicki Minaj number! It should have been a ballad. It should have been Céline. No one knew how to watch or respond to drag in that moment—it was strange for them *and* for me. Eventually, the audience's liquor kicked in, and my next two numbers went much better. Thank god for the children present, who needed the entertainment, and watched me like I was a Disney princess.

The conditions for a performance may not always be ideal, but a little bit of improvisation and reading the room can change all that. You have to be ready to adapt. There's a performance I'll never forget by another queen in Chicago. It was a poorly advertised pride celebration in a little community space. There were thirty seats set out and only ten were occupied, mostly by folks in the lineup. After some cringe poetry and earnest readings, a queen was slated to perform. How is anyone supposed to perform, in broad daylight, for a seated audience of ten, following all this literary business? I felt so bad for her. Cue Katy Perry's "Firework." More cringe? It had all the makings of a terrible number: no stage, no theatrical lighting, tiny audience, music too low. But she made it *drag*! During that performance, the queen—I wish I remembered her name!!!—came up to every one of us and delivered a verse or chorus while holding our hands, lip-synching directly into our eyes. It was so earnest, so sweet, and so purposeful. She took care of her audience. She was there and present with us. Her drag was *for us*. I'm not one to feel pride during Pride, but I truly loved being gay that day.

I think a lot about audiences when invited to perform. I want to know if there will be queer people there, and if they are used to watching drag. I also want to know if there will be South Asian folks there, or other people of color. How big will the crowd be? What's the seating arrangement? It's helpful to know if the audience is going to be small—I won't be mad but at least I can be prepared. All these things help me craft what I'll say on the mic: instructing people how to tip, explaining what drag is, why I chose that number. I hate when I do a Hindi track for an all-white audience and all they'll say is "That's so beautiful. Thanks for sharing your culture with us." Like, girl, I was doing *much* more than sharing culture or being beautiful. I was being hilarious and sexy! But anticipating an all-white or all-straight audience means I can pivot and do something that allows both me *and* the audience to feel good.

The flip side of this is that I also don't perform songs that fight with my own sensibilities just because my audience might like them. I perform mostly on college campuses. But there's not a muscle in my body willing to perform Chappell Roan even though I know the babies will *Eat It Up*. I tried a Taylor Swift number, and well, major flop. But Lady Gaga, Fergie, and Whitney Houston strike a happy balance, because my body knows how to move with those millennial rhythms and words and feelings. Those songs have been in the air around me for decades now. They feel like me. And the kiddos kind of know the songs; it's what their parents sang to them as lullabies, right?

When it's going to be a mostly South Asian crowd, I *know* they're more likely to know all the words. I ask myself what I can do with the number to tap into their deep familiarity with the track. Do I do the exact steps from the original choreography? Do I surprise them with a little twist? I replace Aishwarya Rai's *diya* in "Silsila Ye Chahat Ka" from *Devdas* with a giant eggplant. Very dumb. But it makes obvious the phallic nature of the lamp in the film. I'll only do this number for a non-desi crowd if I can project the original video behind me, so that they too are in on the joke. Sure, an eggplant is always funny, but my riff on *Devdas* is so brilliant, I don't want to waste a good gag.

Remember, I started performing at *Jai Ho!* There, I did drag for the community rather than a personal, deep desire. My drag is very much outward-oriented, *for my audience* instead of for myself. It's not that I don't love feeling cunty with my winged eyeliner and hourglass figure. The glamour makes me feel powerful. Someone wanting a photo with me makes me feel sexy, even when they have the wrong angle. When taking a selfie with me, always shoot me face-on or from above! Find your light, but don't get in the way of mine! Drag is self-affirming and self-exploratory. Even when it is a gift to *others* it transforms *your* sense of self. But it is performance. It is an expressive practice that reaches outward from the body and the psyche. It has an external impact.

Drag is self-affirming and self-exploratory, but it is performance, an expressive practice that reaches outward from the body and the psyche. It has an external impact.

And so preparing to meet your audience where they're at allows you to then take them on the journey with you.

LOOK OUT FOR YOUR SISTERS!

I talk a lot about getting the audience on your side and in your groove, but you don't always get the mic, especially as a baby performer. I had the mic early on in my career because, as an academic queen, I regularly found myself hosting conference and graduate student cabarets. Who knew this was a genre? I brought the nightclub vibe to the stuffy conference room. Dirty jokes, check. Glitter and sparkle, check. But the one thing I couldn't do was make fun of my co-stars. Shade is expected and highly valued in the drag club. But these were my academic colleagues, in some cases senior professors who might one day be reviewing Dr. Khubchandani's tenure file. Academia has forced my hand as a drag queen; I can't get away with reading other performers, even if love and affection underlies the shade. And alternatively, I don't want to read out people's formal bio. Blech! Boring! So I've focused on making an art of introductions. Researching performers or speakers, getting tidbits about them pre-show, studying their aesthetic via Instagram or once they've arrived at the venue, gleaning what I can from our email or text exchanges.

This goes back to a single moment. Once, I fucked up the pronunciation of a friend's drag name at a queer theatre conference cabaret, and it really stuck with me. I was supposed to be announcing Veronica Bleaus (pronounced "blows") but turned it into "blew-aus." It didn't just ruin the pun; in my embarrassment, I lost my confidence and then lost the crowd as well. It was only for a second, but *I* felt shitty for much longer. I should have asked her name earlier. I should have read through that bio before the show. Messing that up made me resolve to get introductions not only right but beautiful. Personalized intros not only prime the audience to expect great things from other performers, but make the performers feel seen even before their boots hit the stage. It's as important to take care of your fellow performers as it is your audience. Not just introductions, but timely payments, rehearsal scheduling, careful curation of the lineup, arranging for show documentation, purposeful publicity. Drag artists make up a community of performers who are often underpaid, undervalued, and the object of much public derision, so it matters to be good to your fellow artists. And trust me, you'll know *quickly* when there's someone in the community with shitty politics or practices! Gossip travels fast!

> **Drag artists make up a community of performers who are often underpaid, undervalued, and the object of public derision, so it matters to be good to your fellow artists.**

So many people have taken care of me. When I enrolled in *Drag Class* at Rain in Austin, I learned how much interpersonal care drag involves. *Drag Class*, created and run by Sabel Scities, was a ten-week competition at a nightclub in which amateur artists were paired with experienced performers to develop their drag. Enrolling was something I did *for me*, to step up my drag, to invest in it as a craft, to learn to approach drag through the nightclub and not only academia, to do drag every week and not just once in a while.

During *Drag Class* I learned so much about making material resources more accessible. My mentor Rhonda Jewels took me to thrift and beauty supply stores I would never have found on my own. Sabel Scities integrated her own wigs, dresses, DVDs, and choreography into the challenges so she could spread the wealth. A Black queen on the judging panel pulled me aside—I was the darkest contestant—to reveal the secrets of banana powder to me. I learned how to ask for help from my own friends: Robert taught me how to use a sewing machine, and Johnny taught me how to open my throat—get your mind out of the gutter—in order to sing live! My fellow competitors and I cooked dinner together so we could get to know each other better.

People shit on competition, especially drag competitions: "We shouldn't be pitting queer people against each other." But *this* competition—from which no one was eliminated—was truly transformative in teaching me that drag grows when it's done with others. The judging process, unlike the heavily edited judging that we see on *Drag Race*, was an opportunity to receive constructive criticism on my drag, and to see how my drag was interpreted alongside other *kinds* of drag. This competition gave me structure and community.

SOME NUGGETS

OK. Writing is so hard. I'm tired. How does Dr. Khubchandani do it? Can't this be an audiobook where I just talk and don't have to type? My nails have been filed down to nubs from all this clickety clack. Oof! Here are some quick things before I go.

Makeup: When blocking eyebrows, really get the glue *underneath* the hair and against the skin, before flattening it down. Also let the glue dry before applying another layer.

Wigs: Don't cut down all the way to the edge of the lace. Having some lace helps you glue the wig down, re-pin it to a wighead when you need to restyle, and gives a little grip to the wig when it's on.

Body: Hip pads! So many off-the-rack feminine outfits are cut with the expectation of an hourglass figure and so they would droop on me. But hip pads fill them out beautifully! Generally, in addition to garments, think about body shape. That realization came late for me, but has changed so much.

Dress: Color! Black is *so* safe. But it really is *the* go-to for baby dragons, and I hate it. It doesn't catch light on stage; details are washed out. Try on color. Also think about how you can play with transparency, texture, and shine. Organza, velvet, and sequins may feel a bit beyond your everyday wardrobe, but they hit differently when under theatrical lights, so be adventurous.

Lights: I always let my lighting designer know that I want warm white light on my face at all times. I don't spend hours on my makeup for it to be washed out by a pink spotlight. My facial features are not typically feminine, so when the makeup is washed out by colored light, then I just give boy. I've performed in many classrooms and conference halls which means I've encountered too much transphobic overhead lighting. If there's no theatrical lighting available, buy a camping light to use as a spotlight. Designate a friend to hold it and light you through the show.

Stage: Get on the stage beforehand. It may be slipperier than you expected. There may be parts the light doesn't hit—you want to avoid those. If there's no stage, then plan on working your way through the audience. Speaking of working your way through the audience, go out and get those tips! Don't wait for them to come to you.

Tipping: The more numbers you do in the show, the longer your number, the more opportunity and obligation the audience has to tip you. If you like to have everything choreographed beforehand, don't forget to leave in a little time for some crowd work and tip collecting.

Prep: Rehearse. Feel prepared. Know your lip synch. Actually try out the costume reveal beforehand. I have left so many numbers to the last minute and run into costume flubs because of it. I didn't realize how satiny a new set of gloves were, and how hard they made it to unbutton my coat during the number. Improvising is my favorite part about performing, but it only goes well when I've prepared enough and feel confident enough to make shit up.

OK children, aunty is out. Go be a drag queen, king, thing, bing, bang, bong, sing, sang, song! And if you need more advice, contact my agent.

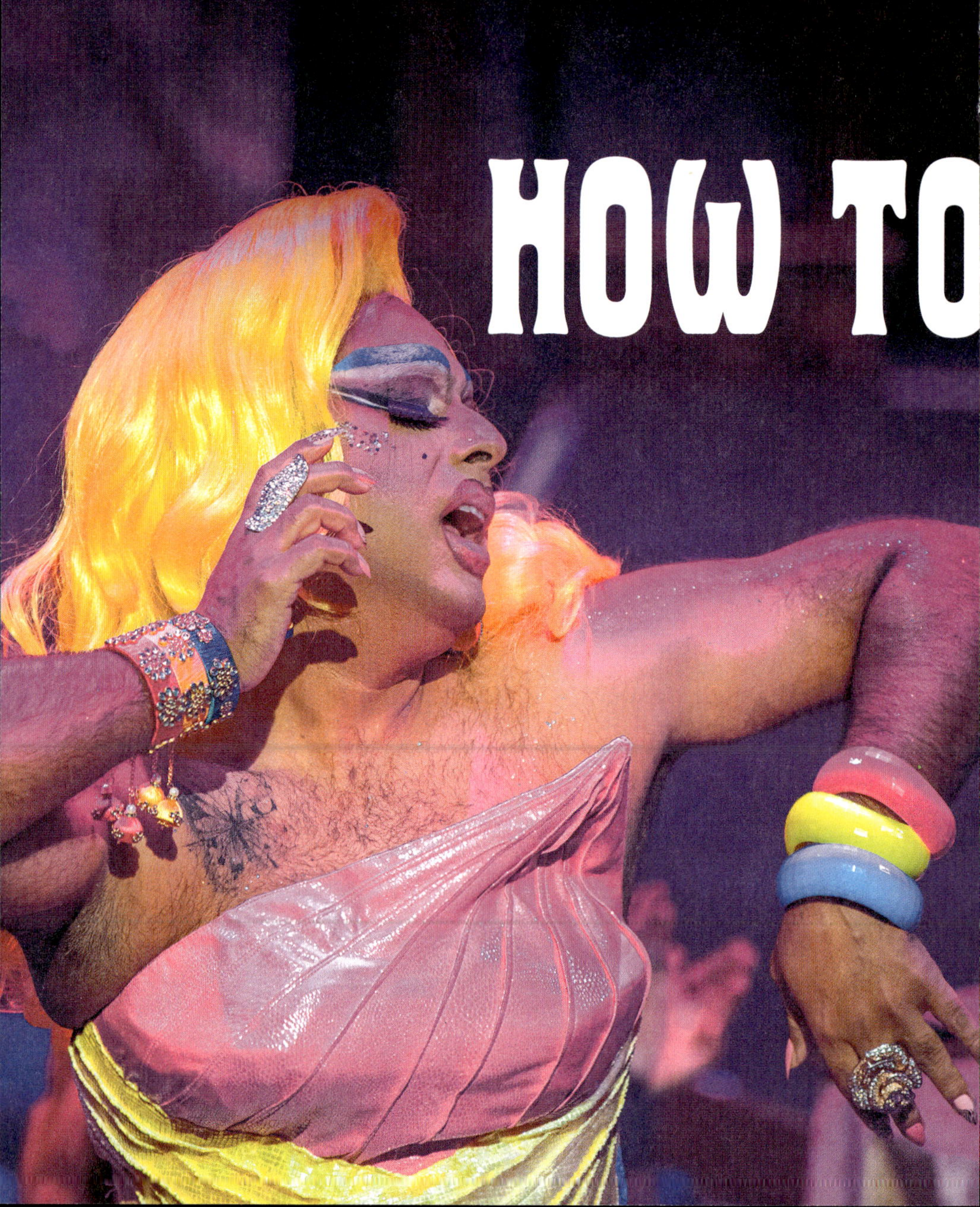

HOW TO

Hi LaWhore.
Received your chapter. Loved it.
I think it fills in some of the gaps
about what exactly drag is
Or at least how you understand it

thanks Dr. K
got a bit long. I got tired.
Rushed end.
Hope that's ok

No, no. That's great
I like how you end with all
those instructive suggestions
Clear and direct
I think I should build the next
section around instruction
On teaching

What about teaching?

About how drag offers tools
to navigate the classroom
Like when you visited my classes

dont forget Drag Class
Austin.

Yes. Makes sense.
What I learned from learning drag as well
Thanks for the suggestion

Always! 💋

BACK TO SCHOOL

When I was in Austin for my postdoctoral fellowship, I lived a stone's throw from the small strip of gay bars on Fourth Street. On Sundays, Oil Can Harry brought in the Ru-Girls to perform alongside their local cast. On Thursdays, Rain hosted amateur strip night, where straight University of Texas students twerked in their ankle socks and checkered boxers. The cursed bar in between Oil Can Harry and Rain that kept getting shut down was great for dancing. The elaborate flashing dance floor was a disco delight. Rumor had it that there used to be small sharks swimming beneath the transparent dance floor who kept dying because of the intense sound waves. Dark! I had never lived in such proximity to gay bars before, and I loved to pop in on a weeknight. The good drag, the weird drag, is always on weeknights. One Tuesday, I stumbled into *Drag Class*, a competition styled as a classroom in which the participants had mentors who helped them complete weekly assignments issued by the show's host. That night, I witnessed baby drag artists showing off their "homework" to the judges. Delightful! Awkward! Genius! I made sure I came back for the next one, which it turns out was the last session of the semester: graduation! And the crowning of the winner!

When I saw fliers for *Drag Class, The 2nd Semester*, I had to enroll. Challenges at *Drag Class* included: taking home a kite, creating a hat out of it, and styling that hat with an outfit for a runway walk; learning choreography on the spot and re-performing it; taking home a DVD from host Sabel Scities's collection and creating a spoken-word lip synch out of it; and writing and performing a song parody. Each class brought in a panel of regular and guest judges—local drag queens, makeup artists, burlesque performers—who gave us feedback on each section: homework presentation, in-house challenge, and final runway. We were graded on each assignment and our grades were tallied for the finale.

Drag Class was a revelation. Over the course of that ten-week competition, I learned that drag was not simply a social practice in queer spaces, but also a highly structured and systematically taught artform. This should not have come as a surprise. My first book *Ishtyle* argues that nightclubs are sites of cultural pedagogy, where you're both implicitly and very explicitly told what to wear, what music to dance to, how to flirt, how to smell. But Austin was my first opportunity to be deeply immersed in drag worlds, to engage them with the same rigor that I did as a clubgoer. Before long, I was exposed to drag economies, ethics, and education. *Drag Class* truly felt like school: take-home assignments, in-class challenges, and a final runway every single week. We actually had to do homework that involved both research and making, and present it "in class" every Tuesday night. When asked to perform a celebrity impersonation, I had to research an icon in order to stage her. Studying Cher, Nicki Minaj, and Rihanna so that I could lip-synch their tracks for different challenges taught me how they hold breath in their bodies, the bodily grammars they inhabit to create fabulous worlds, the showy audacity with which they navigate a patriarchal entertainment industry. I had *just* finished my PhD and here I was a student again.

I learned that drag was not simply a social practice in queer spaces, but also a highly structured and systematically taught artform.

> **Drag has shown me that teaching is performance, a curatorial exercise involving choices about aesthetics, time, bodies, and space that is dynamic and responsive to all those present.**

Drag Class came at a crucial time for me. I was transitioning out of a PhD and slated to move into a full-time faculty role. Witnessing the nightclub as a site of pedagogy, and more specifically experiencing the very generous, dynamic, and embodied pedagogy that nightlife traffics in, radically transformed my teaching practice. It's not that I hadn't taught in drag before, but *Drag Class* made clear the efficacy of teaching in drag. I also learned how to transmit drag. *Drag Class* provided a model for "Critical Drag," a class I teach that mentors students in developing drag personas and lipsynch performances. The class leads students through both improvisatory and pre-scripted exercises that help them flesh out their persona and aesthetic. In the class, they refer to me as Professor Vagistan, and to each other by their drag names.

In this chapter, I want to explore what arriving to class *in* drag has taught me about the craft of teaching, how *Drag Class* theatricalized the act of teaching for the nightclub, and how "Critical Drag" has adopted these lessons to scaffold a drag pedagogy. Teaching is not simply a practice we do by rote because it works. Rather, drag has made apparent that teaching is performance, a curatorial exercise that involves making choices about aesthetics, time, bodies, and space that is dynamic and responsive to all those present.

DR. VAGISTAN, IF YOU'RE NASTY

"Critical Drag" is not the first time LaWhore taught for me. Since graduate school, I have been showing up to my undergraduate seminars in drag. While teaching an undergraduate cultural studies class titled "Bollywood Dance" at Northwestern, I wanted to show my students the fabulous queer choreographies of desi drag queens I had seen in nightclubs. But my field sites did not permit videography, and the internet was not yet brimming with queer South Asian content as it is now.

Bollywood Dance: Film Dance and the Live Body

NORTHWESTERN UNIVERSITY, SPRING 2013

Monday May 13: Gender, Sexuality, Erotics

Before class, read:
Morcom, "Indian popular culture and its others"
Nijahwan, "Excusing the female dancer"
Athalye, "Bar on Chikni Chameli and Munni"
Dudrah, "Queer as desis"

Before class, watch: "Kajra Re," "Munni Badnaam," "Chikni Chameli," "Mere Angne Mein," "Chaiyya Chaiyya," "Sajna Ve Sajna"

In class: Lecture—excerpts from instructor's research

So for "Gender, Sexuality, Erotics" week, seven weeks into the ten-week quarter, LaWhore Vagistan arrived to teach my class instead of me. This was an innovative strategy born out of necessity and lack, brimming with messy possibility. I designated someone else to set up the projector in the dance studio that day so that LaWhore could arrive late, once most of the class was present and settled. "Hi! I'm sorry, Kareem isn't well. Diarrhea, it seems. So, I will be your instructor. My name is LaWhore Vagistan! You can call me Professor Vagistan."

LaWhore lectured on item girls, wet saris, and queer nightclubs. Instead of explaining the appeal of desi drag, she demonstrated it. Rolling on the ground in a sari promising to come unpleated in front of my students, while also explaining the sexual politics of the sari in Hindi cinema, I found a certain success in my students' bewildered expressions, not unlike my own when I first attended *Desilicious*. They were seeing me anew and learning to see a heteronormative film genre with fresh eyes. An Indian woman remarked, "I know all these songs. I know these moves. But I don't know how to watch them on your body."

LaWhore defamiliarizes the classroom space, prompting students to reach in new directions to interact with class materials. You know how you can *feel* the air change when you bring in a guest speaker? Especially mid-semester when the classroom environment has become a little bit tedious? Arriving as LaWhore is like being *my own* guest speaker. After LaWhore did her lecture, I de-dragged and sat with the students for a post-performance/lecture discussion. They opened up about their many encounters with drag, including their familiarity with dressing up and transforming gender for high school theatre productions. Bringing my own chaotic daytime drag to the classroom allowed students to place themselves in a drag spectrum and to see Bollywood through a queer lens.

When LaWhore teaches for me, I always keep it a surprise. Even if I've planned her appearance since the first draft of the syllabus, I don't name her arrival on the document. I need to give myself the option to not wake up so early and get into drag on a weekday morning. Until recently, I needed to designate four hours to get into full drag—I've gotten it down to a neat ninety minutes. Not announcing her visit in advance leaves room for spontaneity; LaWhore can show up when she's needed. When class morale was at an absolute low—in 2016, when Trump won the presidency, and in 2020, when the Biden-Trump vote count held us all in suspense—LaWhore arrived to lighten the mood. At Zoom University, during the Covid pandemic, LaWhore belted Lizzo with my students, a karaoke sing-along that allowed us all to feel a little bit happier in the midst of a global crisis.

You know how you can *feel* the air change when you bring in a guest speaker? Arriving as LaWhore is like being *my own* guest speaker.

What takes me by surprise *every single time* LaWhore teaches my class is that students are ready to play along. They will call her Dr. Vagistan and refer to me in the third person. Drag reminds me that students are ready to play in the classroom. I'm not advocating play for play's sake; I don't see my role at the university as an entertainer. That's a role queer people and people of color are too often asked to assume, and I'm wary of reproducing those hierarchies, of falling into that trap. But I do think that fun is a valuable pedagogical tool when it asks students to approach scholarly material anew.

Every single time LaWhore teaches my class, students are ready to play along. They call her Dr. Vagistan and refer to me in the third person. Drag reminds me that students are ready to play in the classroom.

Beginning the semester as Professor Khubchandani, and not Kareem, is one of my ways of insisting on the seriousness of the work we do. I'm the kind of professor who insists we begin with the assigned materials, working to understand, interpret, and exhaust them before generalizing their themes or inviting the personal into our discussion. When LaWhore arrives, she takes the same approach—"Professor Vagistan"—but radically reorients and enlivens it, poking fun at Dr. Khubchandani, revealing the theatrical nature of social and institutional roles while also making clear how adhering to roles can actually be useful.

This is something LaWhore takes into her nightlife performances as well: "My name is LaWhore. Professor Vagistan if you're nasty. How are you doing tonight? [audience woos] Oh you can do better than that. That was definitely a C minus! I see a lot of overachievers in the room, and I know you want that A plus. So I want to hear what an A plus sounds like. I want to feel those screams in my Vagistan! [Insert name of nightclub/party/college] how are you doing tonight?" The ruse of the classroom, the grade, the rubric gives people structure and motivation to engage, to be together.

Appearing in the classroom in drag makes especially clear to me that gender and appearance have everything to do with how my students learn. Research in education has demonstrated that women, especially women of color, are treated and evaluated much differently than their white men counterparts are. This means that women, especially early career professors or women who "look young," feel they must dress in ways that desexualize their bodies and make them appear older in order to be taken seriously. I know all this. I know that the way I present my body, race, gender through dress, makeup, skin, facial hair, voice are all shaping how students interpret my social positioning. With this come their implicit biases about how rational my thinking is, how emotionally driven I am, how nurturing or understanding I'm likely to be. This then shapes their interpretation of the work I've assigned them even though it was written by someone else entirely. I know that being a queer person of color makes *some* students feel safe. Others are suspicious of the fact that I'm willing to share queer-of-color knowledge with white, straight, or cis people. My body is always being related to the material I teach, and I never have the privilege of neutrality that a white man educator does.

I know all this because I've read it. But when I bring a *different* avatar into the classroom from the one I usually inhabit, I encounter a visceral reminder of how *the body* itself makes the difference. When students approach LaWhore differently from the way they interact with me, it enfleshes theories of pedagogy. Students take in knowledge through bodily cues. Some are intimidated by LaWhore; others are affectionate toward her. I've seen students who were perfectly comfortable talking to me clam up when LaWhore asked them questions. I've also seen students who barely spoke in my sessions come alive with a thousand ques-

Students take in knowledge through bodily cues. Some are intimidated by LaWhore; others are affectionate toward her.

tions for LaWhore—makeup tips, opinions about *Drag Race*, music trends. She creates a distance that allows some students to relinquish formality with "the professor" and others to fall into formality with "this stranger." And when I come back to class after LaWhore has visited, there is an eagerness to continue the game, to tell me what I missed, what LaWhore said. To experience my students differently leaves me acutely aware of how much their perception of me—my identities, my body—structure how they relate to me and therefore the material. Again, these are things I know in theory, but to feel them in such embodied ways motivates me to more carefully consider how I bring myself into the room every day.

One time, LaWhore was feeling especially brazen: "I'm very happy to be substituting for Dr. Khubchandani's class at your prestigious institution. But I've never met him. I was wondering if you could do your best impersonation of him?" In this exercise, students essentially rehearsed my own pedagogical style, mapping it onto their bodies. It was certainly very funny to watch, and I had to work hard to keep a straight face. But the thing that got me every time was when they mimicked me trying to put them into breakout rooms on Zoom. Counting the number of people present, then struggling with the math, then trying to designate who was in what room. It was mortifying to watch it re-enacted back to me, and absolutely hilarious. LaWhore definitely had a good laugh at my expense.

This moment taught me that students are watching, observing, absorbing—not just the class content, but my body, habits, tendencies, and style as well. There are mundane things I do that annoy them, and others that comfort them. These too are central to *how* they learn. My students' responses to LaWhore teach me

My students' responses to LaWhore teach me that if I don't take performance seriously then I might not be putting my time and space with my students to their best use.

that if I don't take performance seriously—embodiment, staging, the quality of light and sound, the balance of improvisation and preparation—then I might not be putting my time and space with my students to their best use.

I know that race, gender, ethnicity, age, accent, voice might already be determining the way my students see me and engage with materials in my class. They are not asking white cis-men professors to be more vulnerable in class, to play more games in class, to talk more about their personal life and feelings, the way they have asked me and my queer-of-color and women colleagues to. And let's not forget questions of academic discipline. The academy is structured to devalue the arts and humanities, to make them boxes to check in an increasingly professionalized curriculum. Given these dynamics, it makes sense that students show up in my classes expecting our work together to be easy, or fun, or therapeutic. And it can be. But the expectation that it *will be* calls on some of us in the academy to perform *for* students, to play roles that we were not hired to take on: therapists, mothers, social workers, comedians, clowns. It's precisely for these reasons that I *must* draw on performance to compensate for—or when convenient lean into—these biases and unfair expectations. My awareness that I am compelled to perform gives me the impetus to take control of the performance.

Teaching in the university classroom as LaWhore is an opportunity to transgress some of the mundane restraints I place on myself as a teacher; she is cattier, blingier, more sarcastic, more animated than I ever am. Lord knows I've wanted to roll my eyes, lash out, or throw my pencil case dramatically in class. I am most sorely tested when students haven't done the reading but still bullshit in class about something they don't know, taking up space and wasting everyone's time simply to show that they're "participating." Although my students tell me I don't have a great poker face, I at least try to resist some of these impulsive behaviors. But foul-mouthed, cleavage-baring quick-lipped, bit-of-a-bully LaWhore gives me momentary license to not coddle my students, to be critical of them in ways that feel unburdened of *certain* social roles (like the caretaking queer-of-color professor that queer and trans students flock to on an oppressively straight campus), while also trying on some new ones.

THE NIGHTCLUB IS MY CLASSROOM

Drag Class is one of the hardest things I've ever done. When I arrived on day one with a sequin jumper, bronze leggings, mealy eyebrows, and a shake-and-go wig, I thought I looked stunning. But as soon as I saw the other contestants, also amateur performers, my confidence fell. I felt the poverty of my makeup, styling, and posing skills. As mentors were paired with mentees, I could tell no one wanted me as their drag child. I later found out my instincts were right about this when one of the other drag mentors tried to sabotage my relationship with my mentor Rhonda Jewels by telling me so. But *Drag Class* gave me my *She's All That* fantasy. LaWhore experienced a veritable glow-up. Learning to blend and contour! Learning to pad! Absolutely life-changing!

Taking part in *Drag Class* was an important reminder that learning happens outside the classroom. Not just learning. Structured, artful pedagogy happens outside the classroom. This was a simple, but profound, realization. *Drag Class* taught me what else a classroom could look and feel like. In addition to homework and feedback and instruction, a classroom can include light-up checkered dance floors, disco balls, loud music, and community! I learned, over and over again, that the classroom was indeed an aesthetic performance space that could be

Drag Class taught me that in addition to homework and feedback, a classroom can include light-up checkered dance floors, disco balls, loud music, and community!

used creatively and differently each time. The fact that this nightlife competition was staged as a class pushed contestants to focus on improving every week, rather than simply delivering on the brief. Sabel Scities, playing the role of "instructor" rather than "emcee" or "judge," fostered a feeling of safety. Each performer had a mentor assigned to them. This made it clear that it was OK to not know; someone was present to help you grow. Right next door at Oil Can Harry, the weekly competition was *Drag Survivor,* with a much more cut-throat ethos and weekly eliminations. At *Drag Class,* no one was eliminated and everyone had the chance to improve.

I had many epiphanies in *Drag Class.* The first was that sharing your work benefits everyone. Every week in *Drag Class* we all witnessed each other's performances and saw how we all had interpreted the same brief. I was amazed by how much I learned *from my peers,* from the unexpected and kooky ways they interpreted the same assignment I had spent the entire week working on. When we had to restyle one of Sabel's old wigs, I went out and bought neon extensions to weave the short black wig into a tall up-do, whereas another contestant didn't even wear it on her head but integrated it into her costume!

This ethos of camaraderie and peer exchange experience has inspired me, in my current role, to create assignments for my own courses in which students share work with each other. In some undergraduate classes, I require students to review each others' submissions before class. I love this exercise because it cultivates a culture of mutual admiration and respect, as students begin to see each other as thoughtful researchers and co-thinkers. There is always a lot of gratitude for how much they learned from each other. I find that this format also changes the quality of writing students produce. When you're writing for your instructor, you assume she has the interpretive tools to decipher your particular blend of ideas. But when you're writing for peers, you're writing for someone who isn't as deeply versed in the material, so there's a desire (pressure?! obligation?!) to be more generous and accessible.

In addition to realizing that sharing your work with your peers benefits everyone, I also learned how valuable public feedback is. The *Drag Class* judging panel was simply incredible. Terrifying. But incredible. LaWhore has never gotten so much feedback, before or since: the references people saw in her style; the colors that looked good on her body; the products that brought out her lip better; the fact that she relied on leggings and pants instead of dresses. I would *never* have noticed my tendency to wear pants had it not been pointed out; sometimes you're just not primed to examine your own patterns. Given this consistent feedback, my mentor Rhonda put LaWhore in a black lace dress one day—LaWhore kept calling it a gown because it felt so fancy to her—and gave her a black lip. It was so severe, so stunning. She could never have arrived at such a sultry look without the feedback, encouragement, and mentorship of the judges.

All the feedback I got in *Drag Class* was impactful. But I learned *even more* from all the feedback that the judges gave my peers. I learned that if the audience can see obvious undergarments, it interrupts the fantasy you're trying to create with your look. I learned that audiences can tell when you don't know the words to a lip synch (this was pre-Valentina!) and so you should always learn your lyrics. I learned that having a recognizable visual aesthetic (one contestant wore newly thrifted bridal gowns every week) is endearing because it teaches the audience who you are—it gives you an aesthetic stamp—but it can also function as a crutch. And yes, we've all heard a version of these critiques on *Drag Race* as well, but it is actually very helpful to hear them said about a garment right next to you, about a performance you witnessed only five minutes ago, live and in person.

I was very moved by the public nature of the judges' feedback and have adapted that to my own teaching. Where relevant, I've made all my critical responses (except grades) to students' work available to the entire class. That way students can see what kinds of patterns they're falling into if a lot of them got the same critique, and can step in to support each other if they have the tools to help. Alternatively, after I've sent out comments and grades, I ask students in class, "Was there any feedback I gave you that you think might also benefit your classmates as well?" Making student work *and* my criticism of it more open and available allows for a more transparent classroom.

By theatricalizing the classroom, *Drag Class* split open the private space in which we're habituated to think learning happens and made obvious the "roles" we play in the classroom.

By theatricalizing the classroom, *Drag Class* actually split open the private space in which we're habituated to think learning happens and made its guts public. It cast classrooms as physical spaces that can be repurposed and reimagined. It made obvious the "roles" we play in the classroom. It put on display those parts of learning we tend to privatize: homework and feedback. So even though I research performance, art, design, being a student of *Drag Class* actually pushed me to use those tools in my pedagogy, and not simply to teach *about* them.

CRITICAL CONDITION

The judging panel at *Drag Class* was hugely helpful. But there were also days when the judges simply hated a look, were confused by LaWhore's body hair, or showed disinterest in someone's pop culture references. Their feedback was "No, girl!" or "Hated it!" or "Meh." Those were hard days. Negative criticism is not bad, but when it is *so* unspecific, it gives us nothing to build on and leaves us unmoored.

Criticism is its own art. And often, I find, we don't have the words to explain what we love or hate about drag. I developed "Critical Drag" as a hybrid cultural studies and performance class. The "critical" in the title names on the one hand the urgency of drag, of studying drag, in a historical period that undermines the artform through attacks on drag story hours, transphobic legislation, and bans on public performance. The word "critical" also suggests that critique is important both *in* drag and *to* drag. Critique *in* drag means that drag is an artform that can be used for the purposes of social critique. At the same time, critique is important *to* drag in the sense that I want students to be able to speak analytically about what they see happening in drag performances and how it relates to structures of power. To be able to watch drag and say more than "yaas" and "werk"—not that these are not powerful affirmations—and to afford drag the purposeful analysis that it deserves. Teaching "Critical Drag" was exactly what led me to write *Decolonize Drag*. I wanted people to see how powerful drag could be as a medium to speak back to systems of power, and I wanted to give others a language to speak *about* drag with care and precision.

I was intent on getting students to collaboratively develop a productive and performance-enhancing environment in the classroom through mutual critique. Critique can be a gift, but it is not always taught. "Critical Drag" doesn't start with performance; we start with performance criticism. Early in the semester, we spend time discussing the techniques and technologies of drag. Technologies are the materials that drag artists put on or take off, highlight or subdue on the body in order to tell a story and build a world; techniques are the ways they manipulate their body and its accompanying technologies.

We watch clips of the queens' entrances on *Drag Race*, and students call out the various technologies they use: "Wigs!" "Heels!" "Makeup!" Then we watch the same clip again, and I invite students to look at those same technologies, but describe them more closely: "A fluffy lavender wig." "Black patent, open-toed heels." "Overdrawn burgundy lips." Once we have this list, I ask them, "OK, so what does wearing black, patent, open-toed heels do? What does it reference? What does that make you feel about the person wearing them?" "It feels stripper-y." "Dominatrix!" "Power." "Darkness." "OK, so what story is being told when she has on those heels, with a black body suit, red lip, blonde hair?" Forcing students to take in the materiality of drag through its smallest component parts and then reassemble them alongside their social meanings gives them tools to go beyond loving or hating a look. Instead, they can grasp what the look *wants* to do, and then evaluate if it was successful at doing it.

We do the same task with techniques. "Posing, hip out." "Flirtatiously batting her eyelashes." "Speaking at a high register." "Crossing ankles, left over right." By this round, the adjectives and adverbs are abundant. This is an important moment in which students see that drag is not simply about a visual accomplishment of gender, but is a fleshy, bodily artform that erupts when technology and technique interact with each other.

As they learn to describe technologies and techniques, *and then* explain how the mobilization of both impacts their experience of the performance, students develop a valuable set of tools for performance criticism. "This is the specificity I want you to bring to evaluating your colleague's performances," I tell them. "First reiterate what you witnessed, in order to explain why you experienced it the way you did." So even when students don't already know the track someone is lip-synching to, or they don't get a specific reference in the costume, they can still detail and process their experience of the performance. This makes it almost impossible to take the lazy route—"I didn't get it, so I didn't like it."

"Critical Drag" isn't the kind of class that can have prerequisites. I have to assume that students have no background in drag, and get them from zero to a hundred in a semester. Both times I've taught the class, barely a handful of students had performance experience. So how do you get students on their feet, for their very first solo lip synch in front of an audience? This challenge forced me to return to the basics of teaching: how to scaffold learning in ways that allow students to build on previous assignments in order to grow their knowledge and abilities.

I reached into the tools of *Drag Class* once again to solve this problem. One of Sabel's assignments was to perform a celebrity impersonation. For LaWhore, this was a nightmare assignment. Which South Asian celebrities did we have in 2016? Mindy Kaling? Pre-

Nick-Jonas-pre-*Quantico* Priyanka Chopra? Malala? LaWhore very seriously considered doing Malala. She settled on Nicki Minaj. The challenge of doing Nicki came with a number of exciting firsts: first time with pink hair, first time with padded hips, first time lip-synching a rap. Developing this performance meant much more than performing a Nicki song. It required research: her history, her beef with other musicians, her wardrobe. LaWhore fell deep into YouTube holes of podcasts and other interviews. Doing a celebrity impersonation reminded me that you *could* teach an old aunty new tricks, that I could harvest new gaits for my body, new aesthetics for my wardrobe, new gestures, head movements, facial expressions, and mannerisms from closely studying someone else.

Doing a celebrity impersonation reminded me that you *could* teach an old aunty new tricks, that I could harvest new gaits for my body, new aesthetics for my wardrobe, new gestures, head movements, facial expressions, and mannerisms.

For "Critical Drag," I asked students to research an icon that might inform their drag style in an assignment called "Dramaturgy of an Icon." How does the person dress? How do they move on stage? Where did they grow up? How does their music relate to their life story? And so on. Students write essays, which we all read and discuss. After that, I invite them to perform impersonations of their icons—their first embodied assignment for the class.

Coupling the "Dramaturgy of an Icon" with "Performance of an Icon" allowed students to transition from writing exercises to performance early in the semester. It also slowed down the development of that first performance, broke it into study first and embodiment second. Further, it added narrative, affect, and history to what could simply be mimicry. It gave students a *reason* to embody these choreographies, gestures, and lyrics.

Faced with this assignment, several students showed interest in ex-

Critical Drag

TUFTS UNIVERSITY, FALL 2022

Dramaturgy of an Icon: Four-page (double-spaced) researched/descriptive essay

How does a celebrity become a celebrity? You will choose a celebrity who inspires your drag to research. What were their beginnings? How did they achieve iconicity? What are their signature styles of dress, movement, hair, and makeup? How do/did they reinvent themselves? How have they been taken up by fans, politics, and as public symbols? What is most recognizable about them? In addition to the story you want to tell about them and their aesthetics, we'd also like you to spend one page describing a performance of theirs that you think captures their individual style. This essay does not need an introductory paragraph or a thesis statement, but it does require citations of sources used. Please footnote references using Chicago Style, with a full bibliography at the end (bibliography does not count toward page count); academic and popular sources are all welcome. Please upload under the assignments page on Canvas with format: yourname-nameoficon.doc by Friday, September 30, by 5 p.m. so that your colleagues have time to read the essay.

Performance of an Icon: 1.5 mins

This will be a 1.5-minute lip-synch performance tribute to the icon you have chosen. It does not need to replicate one performance of that icon, but should rather function as a tribute to their style. How can you best match their bodily style, hand gestures, facial expressions, the way they hold the mic, their dance moves, how they move their lips, etc.? Given that we may not be the same race as the person we're studying, it is necessary that we understand these performances as tributes, as an honoring of this icon and their individuality, as opposed to enacting a generalized appropriation of racial difference. You will be graded on your physical embodiment of the icon; while you are welcome to use costume and makeup to enhance your performance, this will not count toward your grade. Please upload the MP3 under the assignments page on Canvas with format: yourname-iconclip .mp3.

perimenting with nonnormative and especially nonaggressive masculinities, and wrote about and performed Beck, Kenny Chesney, Usher, Freddie Mercury, and Prince. I never thought I'd see Beck drag in this lifetime. It was shockingly excellent! Others took the opportunity to dive deep into their current obsessions: Carly Rae Jepsen, Lady Gaga, and [*rolls eyes*] Taylor Swift. This was a useful activity to help them harvest techniques and technologies rather than start with an empty slate. It also reflected the culture of celebrity-worship that shapes drag more broadly: the deep investment in gossip, iconography, sartorial style, and (often tragic) life stories that make public figures so compelling to queer and trans people. The debriefs from this slate of performances were especially productive because students had read each other's "Dramaturgy of an Icon" essays and could comment on how their peers translated research into performance. A lot of learning happened *between* students, in the very careful feedback they gave each other, and in the networks of support they developed as they sourced costumes and props from each other's wardrobes.

But even a class this engaged needs a break. And when Professor Vagistan is the one teaching the class all semester long, I can't surprise them with my usual "guest" visit. And so I brought in real guests. Drag king Jayden Jamison brought Trans Tape to class, in order to demonstrate how to safely use tape for chest binding. Scottie Gage, founder of Verna Felton, came in to discuss how his nonprofit is making drag clothing freely available to those who can't afford it. I brought in boylesque performers to offer workshops in masculine comportment, and heels dancers to help students conquer stilettos. Offering them access to Boston's larger drag scene, and bringing that drag scene into my classroom, has given many of them a path into professional performance worlds as well.

PUTTING THE "ASS" BACK IN "CLASSROOM"

Both times I taught "Critical Drag," the class became the students' in many ways. As we approached the final public showcase, they made their own fliers, filmed a trailer, and even arranged for video and photo documentation. They booked rehearsal spaces and scheduled practices for the group number. They mixed tracks for each other. They sourced props—including a coffin that was famously carted around campus to the performance location and appeared on many Instagram stories that week! Relinquishing control to the class in this way was new to me. Of course, I did still bring my expertise in performance curation and direction to the showcase. For many of my students, the final showcase was their first time in a formal theatre space; they had never attended a technical rehearsal before nor had access to a dressing room. They certainly didn't know the difference between upstage and downstage. Tech and dress rehearsals can be intimidating, exhausting, or simply disorienting, and I found it helpful to explain in advance how and why things would run the way they did.

It's been an important negotiation for me, thinking about how much power I hold onto or let go of as an instructor. As you may have gathered, even though I always begin the semester with a measure of formality, a lot of students will eventually turn me into a familiar subject, calling me Kareem instead of Dr. Khubchandani. I understand the calls for a democratic and even abolitionist classroom in which there are no hierarchies between students and their professor. But, in my experience, relinquishing authority is not even an option when I barely have any to begin with. As a queer person of color, students see me as a peer from day one. But, to return to what I said earlier about exerting control over the roles we are bound to perform, by developing awareness of *how* students see me, I can work carefully to secure our relationship in ways that are productive for us all. Roles are fictions; they offer comfort and continuity as much as they allow for play. This is why I allow students to call me "Aunty," to see me as the familiar authority, one who is simultaneously caring and bossy. And sometimes aunty has to intervene.

Roles are fictions; they offer comfort and continuity as much as they allow for play. This is why I allow students to call me "Aunty," to see me as the familiar authority, one who is simultaneously caring and bossy.

I'm grateful I'm able to teach "Critical Drag," that the university supports this class, given the wickedly anti-trans, anti-drag sentiments in the world. But I was also surprised to see how the conservative discourses around drag shaped my students' approaches to and experiences of their own performances. In the post-performance debrief following our final showcase, a few students mentioned that audience members, their friends and roommates, found some of the performances "sexy" or "hot." Students were disturbed by these comments; they insisted that drag was about gender and not about sexuality. The anti-trans backlash against drag, which casts drag as "adult entertainment" or "sexual performance," has created an environment in which drag is sometimes forced to disavow its many relationships to sex, sex work, stripping, burlesque, go-go dancing, and so on. Mind you, our show had featured many, many garments being taken off to reveal flesh; costumes included harnesses, chaps, fishnets, riding crops, and other kink-subculture items; and several performers had done the Teyana Taylor floor hump. It *was* sexy. It *was* hot.

I'm eager to make room for sexiness, not simply so that students can name it out loud without flinching, but so they can find the words to explain how it brings value to the performance. But I also had to speak up and remind my students about who gets excluded when we accept these lines, lines defined by the conservative right in particular. I inventoried the damage that anti-drag rhetoric had done in our own classroom, and offered a rebuttal. No Socratic method. No gentle feedback. Just a firm statement of what is actually what. To be honest, I don't know exactly how it landed, but it felt urgent.

> I'm eager to make room for sexiness, not simply so that students can name it out loud without flinching, but so they can find the words to explain how it brings value to the performance.

This hot take on the last day of class was informed by Aunty's lifetime of experience *doing* drag. I didn't used to feel sexy in drag. I came to drag, as I've said, for community. I developed performances that traded on references and aesthetics my audiences would know and adore. I leaned into camp and fun and play. One night, after a *Drag Class* show, I was on the patio of Rain, about to cross back into the dance floor area. An older man approached me. He told me I was beautiful. He made clear he'd be interested in having sex with me; money seemed to be on the table. I had *never* imagined someone could find my drag look and body beautiful, or even sexy, sexy enough to pay for. But that moment shifted my self-perception. It gave me a glimpse into how I *could* be perceived. It gave me permission to want to look and feel sexy when I'm getting into drag. Now, when chasers appear in LaWhore's Instagram DMs with a "Hi Aunty"—this is now a regular occurrence—she's rather pleased. So when students insist that drag isn't supposed to be about sexuality, I lean into this memory to remind myself that sexuality has empowered my drag practice.

If I bring drag into the classroom, I have to invite sexuality in, too. As my colleague Laurence Senelick has argued, performance traditions that aestheticize gender are imbricated in desire, sexual orientation, sexual expression, and sex work. When I steer students toward a grammar for interpreting drag artistry, I must also give them the language to account for sex and desire. When we don't develop an interpretive language around informal arts—drag, social dance, sex, porn, protest, gossip—we leave them vulnerable to conservative public rhetorics, and we render them devoid of intellectual content. But sex, like drag, is where knowledge is rehearsed, unmade, and created. As I continue to teach this class, I'm eager to make room for sexiness, not simply so that students can name it out loud without flinching, but so they can find the words to explain how it brings value to the performance.

A BAD EDUCATION

Drag reveals that understanding teaching as an artform can be deeply generative. I mean "artform" literally. I put care into the form and design of my classes: the arrangement of space, my delivery, how time is structured, how I dress. Taking a class in drag taught me that structured pedagogy happens beyond the university, including in the nightclub, and that the forms of teaching that happen there could transform more formal classroom spaces. Teaching a drag class myself has taught me that it is possible to bring cultural practices into the academy without sanitizing or straightening them.

A colleague once mentioned—actually she brought it up a few times—that she regularly heard so much laughter and clapping and cheering coming from my "Critical Drag" classroom. Unfortunately, it didn't sound like a compliment. She suggested it was distracting, or perhaps strange. Drag has shown me that laughter and clapping and cheering don't need to be strange to the classroom. Or, to put it differently, drag makes the classroom strange in the best ways possible!

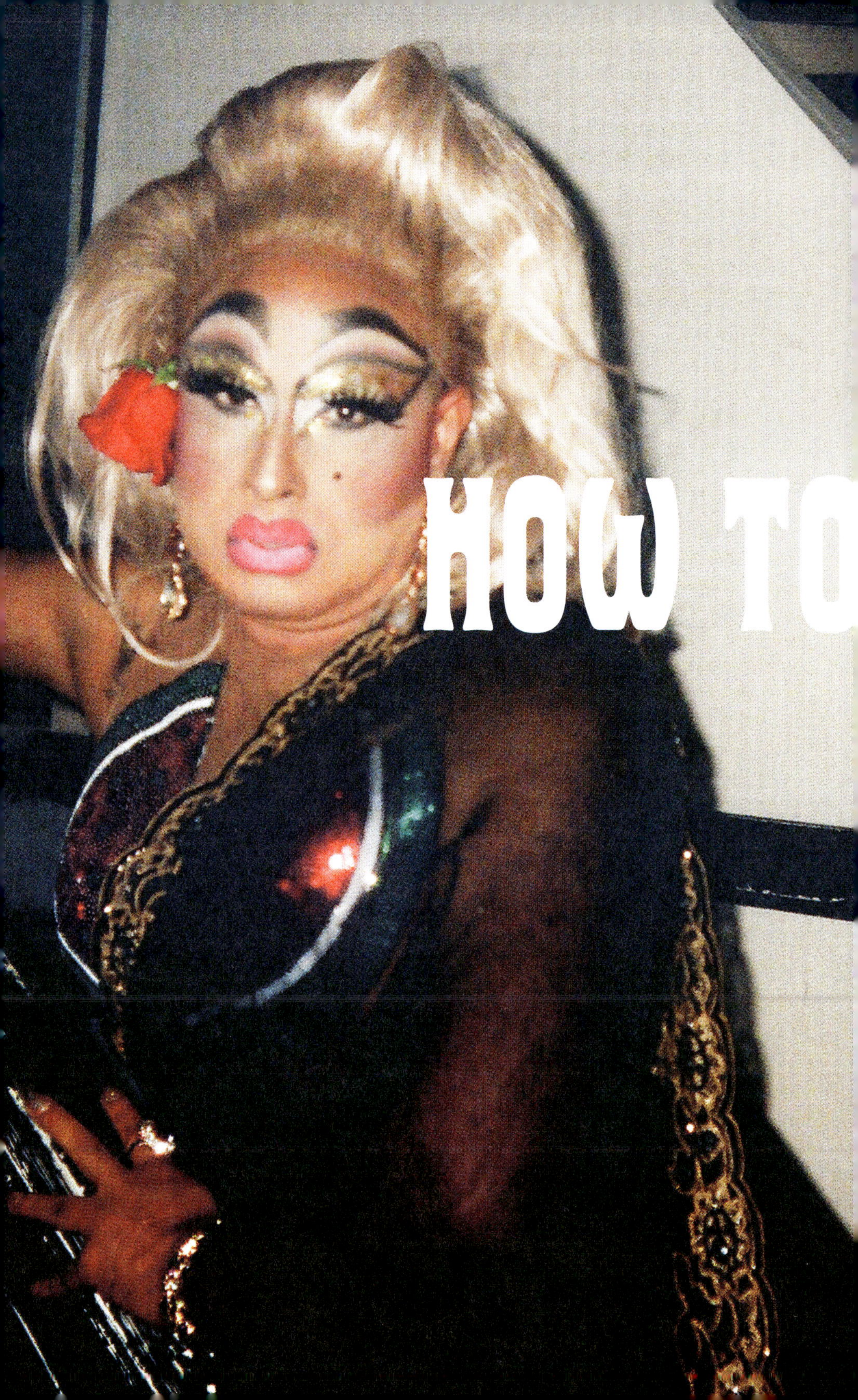
HOW TO

LaWhore Vagistan

CHAPTER FOUR

BE AN AUNTY

omg. is this true? yr colleague
didn't like that you had fun in class?

It was a little
less direct than that.

v passive aggressive 

Very New England 

also, your students don't
want to be sexy?

No LaWhore.
It's more complicated than that.
The way drag has been stigmatized.
They feel they can't risk
staging sexiness.

oof. the children.
they need to learn to be sexy
from their aunties

So show them!
Maybe write your next
chapter about aunties?

but already did aunty ted talk.

Sure. But it was kind of broad.
Maybe focus on drag aunties?

OK good idea. done
🧿🪭💅

My children! Welcome back! I'm glad you've made it this far in the book. Most of you may not know who Dr. Khubchandani is, but I appreciate you bearing with him so that you can reach the important parts of this book: the ones I've written. I'm sure most of you picked up this book because you recognized me on the cover. And for the handful of you who haven't heard about me before, trust me, you have. I get around. If you're trying to place me, you may recall having seen me in the *New York Times*, *Paper Magazine*, or *Vogue India*. As you probably know, I quickly rose to fame with the release of my TEDx talk "How to Be an Aunty." It was filmed in March 2020 at Tufts University, on a Sunday afternoon, the day before the university locked itself down for the first time in the Covid pandemic. What a time that was!

I'm assuming you're very familiar with the video on YouTube? You haven't seen it? Go. Watch. I'll wait.

Welcome back! Did you like my silver and black sari? Matching my silver wig? Yes, I know I'm aging gracefully. When I gave that talk, I was trying to appeal to as wide an audience as possible, trying to show off the aunty as a universal figure. I think it's time to revisit "how to be an aunty." It's time to ask, what does it mean to be a *drag* aunty? I've learned a lot about being an aunty from Professor Khubchandani, his whole Critical Aunty Studies project and all. His message in that project is quite simple: that aunties are exciting figures to think about. They reveal to us a lot about social, economic, and political issues. I tend to agree. I too think of myself as quite an exciting figure! And I have a lot to reveal to you! Wink, wink!

The scholars who write about aunties explain that aunties can be very queer and very trans. If you read all this aunty scholarship Dr. Khubchandani has compiled, there are lots of drag aunties: Filipina Tita Aida, South African Tannie Evita, Sri Lankan Super Aunty, Indian drag queens like Maya the Drag Queen and Pammi Aunty, Indo-Caribbean Tanty Tifa Wine, British Pakistani Aunty Zubaida, and more! This is an alternative to the common trope of evil aunties who are constantly disciplining the youths, reporting back to your mothers that they saw you out with a boy, that you were smoking and drinking in public. What's actually quite funny to me is that even when young people want to criticize aunties, on TikTok or Reels, they'll get *into* aunty drag, wear a dupatta or a caftan or oversize glasses in order to make fun of us. It's like you can't hate us without being *like* us.

I actually found myself in the room one time, when the youths were having their anti-aunty moments! Once, in London, I was invited by a friend to perform at *The Hen-nah Party*. The advertisement said: "a queer alternative to traditional henna nights. Expect live performances, music, dance, poetry, chaat, chat, and of course henna." It was really a sweet event, poetry and fashion and dance and music and me. When the host introduced the night to her very Gen Z audience, she described it as "all the fun of a henna party, but without the aunties!" The shade! Over the night, two different artists read poems that referred to aunties who made them feel some sense of shame: about body hair, about marriageability. Aunties get a bad rap! And I get it! When all aunties care about is who you're going to get married to, and why you've put on so much weight, we become the enemy of young folks ready to fight for their autonomy.

Enter me, sexy in an orange Lycra jumpsuit, copper heels, curly wig. "My name is LaWhore Vagistan, but you can call me aunty." The air left the room. The few laughs were kind of uncomfortable. But I won them over very quickly. I did a medley of songs that ranged from the

1950s to the present, songs they somehow knew because their parents (who are my age!) probably played for them. Aunty was a hit! My bones hurt after, but I was a hit!

When you leave aunties out of the henna party, you risk leaving out the memories and beauty and bodies we bring with us. But also, when you invite aunties in, you risk our melancholy, nostalgia, exhaustion, and paranoia. But it's this accumulation of life lived that makes us so beautiful, no? The very things that make us dangerous are what make us appealing.

Drag is no stranger to aunties. See Season 11 of *Drag Race*, Episode 1. The new contestants are photographed with legends from previous casts. Raja and Manila Luzon, both from Season 3, return to the screen, but this time as aunties. Raja announces herself as aunty upon entering; she makes the choice to age herself, to claim her legendary status by identifying herself as of a different generation. On the other hand, Honey Davenport shrieks when she sees Manila Luzon, her "literal" aunty—Manila was partnered with the late Sahara Davenport, who was Honey's mentor. So, "aunty" can name a family formation, as in the relationship between Manila and Honey. But it also names a more generic elder figure, like Raja, whose impact is felt regardless of her direct relation.

Dr. Khubchandani says a similar thing in his research on aunties. He explains that "aunty" can refer to a wide range of women and feminine figures who occupy social positions at the periphery of nuclear family structures. This means they could be related to you by blood, or they could just be an older figure in your orbit. He also tells us that "aunty" names people who act a certain way, have particular tendencies that verge on "too much." They have too much style or weight or

> **"Aunty" can refer to a wide range of women and feminine figures at the periphery of nuclear family structures, related to you by blood or an older figure in your orbit.**

opinions or secrets. On Season 14 of *Drag Race*, Kerri Colby, Angeria Paris VanMicheals and Kornbread describe themselves as aunties, huddled around their makeup stations gossiping about people's dick sizes—or, as they describe it, "birdwatching." Angeria, Kerri, and Kornbread are certainly too young to be obviously labeled as aunties, but when they do aunty-like things, like birdwatching, it makes perfect sense that they see themselves *as* aunties.

I realize the way I've laid it out makes it sound like drag aunties are everywhere. But in drag discourse, we tend to center drag parents, and rarely aunties. Sure, it's important to credit your drag lineage. But that's the problem: it makes drag a lineage, literally a line, like it's a continuous or straight path into the drag world. But drag journeys are much more diffuse. Someone helps you zip up your gown backstage. Another person gets you your first gig. A TV diva inspires your glamour. Someone else teaches you how to sew, or do hair, or achieve a cut crease. If we talk about drag aunties, in addition to drag mothers and fathers, then maybe we can catch a glimpse into the widely and wildly collective work that is drag!

I'm making aunty-hood sound very attractive aren't I? So let's get into it. What does it take to be an aunty? The good, the bad, the gorgeous.

AUNTIES ARE OLD!

I could tell you about all the ways that I *act* like an aunty, but honestly I *am* an aunty by virtue of my age. In the South Asian drag world, I'm definitely on the older end of working artists. It's not uncommon for Gen Z types to pull an "OMG, it's so good to *finally* meet you. I've been watching your videos since I was a teenager!" or "Wow. I'm in the presence of an *elder*." Might as well cremate me now.

Sure, I *am* old. But embracing age, calling myself aunty, gives me permission to not have to keep up with the youths. I'm allowing myself to *be* old and to *act* old. When I was given a chance to host drag brunch at Sona restaurant in New York City, I instantly knew I wanted to theme the show *Old Is Gold*. Drag brunches are everywhere these days, and they're known for pandering to the straight white lady audience. But this daytime drag phenomenon also creates a space for those of us exhausted by the nightlife scene! You mean I can make my coin and be in bed before nine? Stunning! Drag Brunch joins the tradition of afternoon Tea Dances in making room for other, and older, queer people to participate in the pleasures of nightlife without necessarily being forced into the sometimes stressful conditions in clubs and bars.

Old Is Gold summoned a millennial audience, people who would be attracted to the nostalgia of the 1950s to '80s, rather than the kitsch of the '90s onwards. The golden oldies gave me permission to do slow drag, to wear a gorgeous sari—that doesn't necessarily unravel into a sexy reveal—and glide between the tables, rather than pump out choreography. I put together an ode to Nargis, whose songs were mostly sung by Lata Mangeshkar. Of course, as an over-educated drag queen, I gave the audience a little film history, covering how Nargis carried the burden of embodying "Mother India" and how Lata's shrill voice was forced to represent the virginal sound of an Indian nation. But the dated rhythms meant that I didn't have to keep bopping around the room. I could instead focus on my facial expressions and bring the lyrics to life through sexy lip-bites or beleaguered grimaces. Moving slower also allowed me to collect more tips!

At *Old Is Gold*, I also performed as Helen, Hindi cinema's vamp, who is often written out of a film's storyline by intermission. Helen too has a complicated racial and gendered history with the film industry that I educated the audience about. For us old queens, being on the mic means being a history teacher. Dancing as Helen let me indulge in erratic and jerky movements, rather than a clean eight-by-eight choreography or those vogueing and waacking movements that dominate drag dance these days. Dancing *as* Helen brought a different kind of sensuality to drag.

My "old" drag comes from my aunties. When I dance as Nargis or Helen, I'm also dancing *like* my aunties did. When I was a pre-teen in the late 1980s and early '90s, I'd watch my aunties rehearsing these dances in our family's living room. Sure, they were taking it easy on their bodies with simple moves. But the choreography they borrowed from the screen back then was more gestural and emotional. It wasn't caught up in the five-six-seven-eight that Shiamak Davar introduced with *Dil To Pagal Hai* in the mid-1990s. At shows like *Old Is Gold* I was, in 2024, dancing like my aunties in 1991, who were dancing like film heroines from 1975.

Old drag is an invitation to older folks, other uncles and aunties in the audience, to swing back in time and remember the lyrics, choreographies, costumes, and emotions they hold in their bodies. This doesn't mean we oldies can't marvel at the fabulosity of new drag, of banging remixes and kak-kak-boom choreo! But these different kinds of drag are put in tension with each other all too often. There's a play titled *Tape—aka the Kings of Drag*, produced by Bombay's Patchwork Ensemble, and it stages exactly this generational tension in a drag king club. One performer, who primarily does impersonations of '60s Hindi film star Shammi Kapoor, finds his popularity threatened when he's pitted against a younger drag king who performs as Justin Timberlake. There's another play from the UK, *Miss Meena and the Masala Queens*, about a drag queen being forced out of her nightclub because she does old Bollywood numbers for the queers, and there's a more lucrative clientele of straight men who want to come and watch Punjabi *mujras*, with sexy vexy vigorous choreo. An age-old story! But old and new don't have to be in tension with each other. When I get the opportunity to do my old drag, it feels like a sacred moment to indulge in those memories of gendered

Old drag is an invitation to older folks, other uncles and aunties in the audience, to swing back in time and remember the lyrics, choreographies, costumes, and emotions they hold in their bodies.

beauty that don't often appear in the public sphere, especially in the pop-paced and often very white drag scene. These moments can be really magical.

Being old means I've seen a lot. I have the privilege *and* the burden of living history. And so I get mad, mad as hell, when I see influencers show up on TikTok and Instagram claiming to be the first or the only or the most successful anything. I realize a lot of diasporic queer South Asians, especially those who grew up in predominantly white towns, feel like they are indeed the only or the first whatever. But I was lucky to be surrounded by queer desiness as a teen! At eighteen, I would frequent queer desi parties in New York. The isolation I felt before that dissipated so quickly when I was surrounded by all kinds of bodies, all kinds of genders, all kinds of brown. The queens of those nights—the Sari Sisters, Nina Chiffon, Bijli, Zain—were foundational to my drag. My drag wouldn't exist without them. I won't claim them as aunties—I don't know them like that. I don't know them at all TBH.

But, as an aunty, I'm here to remind the youths that their queerness in not necessarily new. I totally understand how lucrative, socially and fiscally, it can be to market yourself as the only, the first, the newest. But aunty is here to remind you that this only works within an individuating ethos of neoliberalism—you didn't know I knew those words huh?—and its imperative to turn yourself into a commodity. This aunty wants you to think of your drag in collectivity! Share the history. Share the wealth.

AUNTIES HAVE BAD STYLE!

I used to be a member of the Anti-Aunty Club myself. Gasp! I was one of the youths who resented aunties who prioritized marriageable qualities like thin bodies, light skin, caste-compatibility, hairlessness, and heterosexuality. The "When are you getting married, beta?" types. The "Who's going to marry you if you're so [*insert adjective here*]?" types. But, in my twenties, I inadvertently became an aunty because of my style! I wore saris to the nightclub! Becoming an aunty through the sari gave me entry into a different world of fashion and beauty, despite the sari being seen as the wrong fashion for the nightclub.

Saris are famously unfashionable garments for the nightclub. On trips to India in the 1990s and 2000s, fancy Bombay and Bangalore nightclubs would prohibit Indian wear. Uncles and aunties would leave weddings to change out of kurtas and saris, putting on jeans and dress shoes before heading to the club. Saris were cast as impractical and unsexy in the club; pallus are always catching on others' jewelry or cigarettes, or getting stepped on in the crush of bodies. Saris cover up flesh with yards of fabric, and in these spaces you're expected to show as much skin as possible. This isn't to say saris aren't sexy. Receipts: Sridevi's blue chiffon blowing in the winds of an incoming storm, Helen's purple and yellow checks tight around her thighs in a kashta drape, Raveena soaking wet in marigold, Mumtaz in that orange wrap that elongates her legs even though they're never revealed, or Rekha in absolutely *any* sari.

Nightclubs, although they appear to be sites of freedom and escape, are actually quite disciplined spaces with spoken and unspoken rules about how to flirt, dance, groom yourself, and dress.

If you've followed Dr. Khubchandani's research closely, you'll know that he argues that nightclubs, although they appear to be sites of freedom and escape, are actually quite disciplined spaces with spoken and unspoken rules about how to flirt, dance, groom yourself, and dress. Among these explicit/implicit rules is the message that saris aren't the *right* garment for nightclubs, and especially not for drag. Drag calls for corseted hourglass gowns to create snatched waistlines; Lycra leopard leotards for splits and kicks; dresses with gathers, godets, and pleats that extend the twirling body outward; and corseting that pushes breasts up. Saris *can* actually achieve all of these looks, depending on drape and style. But when they are relegated to being "cultural" garments, they don't deliver fabulosity the same way; they signal home and tradition, not escape and futurity. But this is where Dr. Khubchandani's *Ishtyle* research becomes important again. He talks about the possibility of accenting the dominant style of the club, to connect place and nowhere, to bring home to escape, tradition to futurity. Saris allow me to accent the night.

Because the sari can manipulate meaning so nimbly, it is fabulous for the drag stage. It can suggest glamour, but it can also show off power, resistance, class, and sex.

At the beginning of my drag career, I relied heavily on saris. Particularly because they were cheap. And because they fit. Whether thrifted or store-bought, dresses and gowns that served a modicum of glamour were a struggle to find in my size. But the 800-rupee sequined polyester saris I bought on Commercial Street in Bangalore while fabric-shopping with Mum made me feel sparkly, regal, sexy, and expensive at my shows. This is the magic of the unstitched garment. It can be worn by people of many genders, and it can be styled and pleated and draped in ways that signal wealth, or work, or wonder. We tend to consign the sari to suggesting good, compliant womanhood. But for the Gulabi Gang, it marks their defiance of patriarchy. For Pakistani songstress Iqbal Bano it was a protest against militarist nationalism. For porn legend Savita Bhabhi it is a figure-hugging, flesh-revealing garment. Because the sari can manipulate meaning so nimbly, it is fabulous for the drag stage. It can suggest glamour, sure. But it can also show off power, resistance, class, and sex.

Wearing a sari to the nightclub inadvertently made me "Aunty." Aunty fashion is known for doing the "wrong" thing with a sari: sporting it to the gym, pairing it with sneakers, desexualizing it with a cardigan. And this isn't just a South Asian thing. A whole fashion movement known as Auntycore celebrates the contradictions and comfort of aunty clothing—it's just modeled on thin, young bodies. It becomes fashion on those bodies, and old-fashioned or unfashionable on ours. Fifteen years ago, wearing a sari to the club was the wrong thing for me to do but it felt so right. And people started to call me "Aunty."

I leaned into the moniker for *Drag Class* in 2015. The final challenge for the competition was to write and perform a song parody. Singing live is my worst nightmare. I was absolutely paralyzed. Until Johnny said, "Sorry!" "What?" I said. "Sorry! Sari! Sorry! By Justin Bieber. Sorry! Sari!" It was so perfect. The song had come out just the year prior. The lyrics came easily. I was so proud of myself. I even recorded the track professionally in a studio, and subsequently made a music video. "I look best when I'm dressed like an aunty." That was it. Once the video hit YouTube, I was no longer LaWhore. I was "Aunty." Aunty, in a sari, resonated so deeply with South Asian audiences. They loved it. I couldn't shake it, and I didn't want to. Since then, saris are no longer simply a convenient and affordable garment for me to feel fabulous. I continue to wear saris because I enjoy them, because they make my aunty-ness feel complete. Sure, they still feel out of place in the nightclub. The pallu will absolutely get caught on some daddy's leather cuff, and the mucky floor in the bathrooms means I have to drape the garment a bit higher than I'd like. I may not have the right style for the nightclub, but I feel stunning!

AUNTIES TAKE UP SPACE!

During the *Lessons in Drag* show I ask the audience, "What's your favorite aunty attribute?" I'm on my own little quest to counter anti-aunty sentiments, to look for the sweetness, joy, and fun of aunties. When I feel like the audience has worked hard enough to shout out their own answers—she always has safety pins, she has the best gossip, she'll take you to buy a bra—digging past the negative stereotypes to find a little generosity toward aunties, I reveal my own favorite aunty attribute: Zumba.

Barre, Pilates, CrossFit are associated with thin, white, young bodies. But Zumba is a performance-style-cum-exercise-regime that aging, fat femmes find fun and vibrance in even when their bodies are assumed to be domesticated and docile. Zumba lets aunties take up space! Zumba is just one of many collective aunty activities in which women make room for each other's fun. Aunties dancing in China's public squares; aunties overtaking public gym equipment in the park; aunties who turn living rooms into makeup, clothing, or Tupperware shopping experiences. Aunties invent space, especially by misusing it, and I love that!

Aunties take space in order to make space. And aunties make space not simply for individual pleasure, but for collective enjoyment!

I tell the audience I'm about to do Zumba, but I can't do it alone! "I need five volunteers to join me on stage!" The nightclub is about to become *the gym*! What feels most aunty-like in this moment is the invitation. Aunties take space in order to make space. And aunties make space not simply for individual pleasure, but for collective enjoyment!

My favorite model for drag aunty work is curation! Emi Grate, a fellow aunty, is a Burmese drag artist who emigrated—get it? Emi Grate—to the US in 2011. She is a brilliant performer, moving across drag queen and drag king personas, mixing live song, video work, camp, opera, and pop culture in her creative practice. She is a force, developing multiple solo shows based on personal experiences of migration alongside intensely researched music history. Beyond her solo artistry, she began curating a pan-Asian drag revue titled *A+*. Isn't A+ the grade every model minority Asian wants to get? But also A+ as in an extended vision and version of Asian: Asian plus ____.

Emi curates her Brooklyn shows across the lines that carve up Asian diasporas and cartographies; she includes East, Southeast and South Asian artists alongside Pacific Islander, Palestinian, Caribbean, and Blasian artists. Emi is deliberate in inviting bearded drag, drag kings, women queens, and artists who do things other than lip-synch. During the pandemic lockdown, she widened her curatorial possibilities with artists from Singapore, Glasgow, and across the US, including Hawai'i. *A+* makes space for a more expansive notion of Asia and Asian!

Aunty drag makes space for more, invites more people and styles to the table. *A+* does work similar to *Black Girl Magic*, *Nightgowns*, and the *Big Drag King Show*, curating drag for artists and audiences who are often left out of thc popular imagination of "drag." Chicago's The Vixen and Brooklyn's Sasha Velour are both veterans of *RuPaul's Drag Race*. Their shows, *Black Girl Magic* and *Nightgowns* respectively, platform performers who don't receive the recognition they deserve: Black artists, kings, experimental creators, women queens. What's especially amazing about Sasha and Vixen's work is that, even though they are both *Drag Race* alums, it operates outside of the corporate form of RuPaul's drag industrial complex. In 2023, Miss Malice, K.James, and Murray Hill found that New York drag kings were severely under-booked for Pride that year. They pulled together *The Big Drag King Show* in order to showcase how expansive and talented the king community is. These are all expert aunty moves, extending an invitation to those left out of the party to come and revel in the limelight!

Aunties are known for gatekeeping. But Dr. Khubchandani says aunty work can go both ways. Because she works at the fringe of institutions—family, university, nation, nightclub—she has the ability to keep the door shut *or* discreetly unlock it for subversive possibilities to enter. I like to

Aunties are known for gatekeeping, but because she works at the fringe—of family, university, nation, nightclub—an aunty can keep the door shut *or* discreetly unlock it for subversive possibilities to enter.

think that by hosting and curating *Jai Ho!* in Chicago, and subsequently *Dragistan* in New York, I made some room for people other than myself. And since aunties love sending out invitations, then let me say, here and now: You are always welcome in LaWhore's Vagistan.

AUNTIES GOSSIP!

Drag is rarely treated as regulated labor. There are no fixed rates for how much you're paid; contracts are rarely issued for a booking; and (at least in the US) artists are expected to earn the bulk of their compensation as tips. So how do you know whether you're getting a fair deal at a gig? Gossip!

Gossip, rumor, hearsay, they get a bad rap. We think of gossip as secrets whispered between catty gurls who want to see your downfall. But when there are no newsletters, when all we have is consistently transphobic journalism that cares only about *Drag Race*, when gay bars are so often owned by straight men who care more about their profit margin than the treatment of our community, gossip keeps us savvy, and being savvy keeps queens fed! Also, shit-talking feels therapeutic when mediocre, skinny, white performers who knock out the same jokes and the same numbers over and over again get booked and paid and tipped at rates artists of color can't even aspire to. Queens love a bit of spilled tea, we know this! But it's rare that our morsels of information—who is doing the gatekeeping, why this person is no longer being booked, how someone showed their ass—are taken seriously.

During the 2020 Black Lives Matter protests, many reckonings took place in the drag scene, as they did across many other arts and culture institutions. Some were quiet, like white drag artists ceding their hosting gigs to trans women of color. Some were explicit, like bars enacting new policies to be more welcoming and accessible

Gossip keeps us savvy, and being savvy keeps queens fed!

to those they had actively excluded. But in Chicago, a Black Drag March in the Boystown neighborhood, followed by a virtual Black Drag Town Hall, offered a centralized opportunity for Black artists to air their grievances with the city's drag bar owners and producers. Drag work is so disaggregated, the work so informalized, that these kinds of forums, where the community gathers to take stock of power and privilege, are rare. These convenings *should* become the norm. In the meantime, gossip networks transmit difficult community information when public forums like this are so rare.

Drag Twitter is alive with commentary about who the sexual and financial predators are in the community. In some cases, this is handled delicately, because people in the community know that queer and trans abusers will not experience impunity in the way that cis straight men do and in fact experience even more vitriol and violence rather than restorative justice. Accusations dropped into the anonymous digital void can lead to unconscionable harassment. I'll admit, I don't love Twitter and Reddit as gossip venues—too many strangers who may not be reliable links in the chain. But digital gossip *does* allow for some kinds of community care and accountability when there are few to no other structures in place.

Drag Race gossip has become its own cottage industry. Podcasts and vodcasts and live shows invite *Drag Race* performers on to spill the tea about the show's behind-the-scenes happenings: *Roscoe's Viewing Party*, *Sibling Rivalry*, *Race Chaser*, *Very Delta*, *Give It to Me Straight*, just to name a few. *Drag Race* has become so formulaic and slick that there is in fact *so much more to say* about how filming went, how the drama played out, than what appears in the final edit. Queens booking

> *Drag Race* has such a deep impact on both queer and straight people's understanding of queerness, transness, and drag. Gossip has the potential to undo some of the most rigidly overproduced narratives.

tell-all podcasts as soon as their non-disclosure agreements expire is now a given. I'm so here for it. They regularly discuss how heavily manipulated the outcomes of their season were. It's not as if we don't know that is how reality TV works. But *Drag Race* has such a deep impact on both queer and straight people's understanding of queerness, transness, and drag. Gossip has the potential to undo some of the most rigidly overproduced narratives.

Maybe you've seen the meme of Bob and Peppermint on an Instagram Live accidentally mentioning RuPaul's fracking reveal, then losing all composure and falling into fits of laughter at their faux pas. One of my *favorite* internet moments. So good! Clearly they violated a gag order on critiques of Mama Ru! But is this not the joy of gossip? Aunties give breath to the unspoken critiques we have of those in power. And when a little tea gets spilled in public, we finally get to be in on the joke and laugh hysterically too.

AUNTIES OVERFEED EVERYONE!

When my drag mentor Rhonda Jewels picked me up to take me to Emma Sis's house to make pads for *Drag Class*, I felt a little funny. I was going empty-handed to a stranger's house to engage in a task I also felt a little strange about. I wasn't sure I wanted to wear pads—a little too insistent on biological gender, no? Spoiler alert, I love wearing pads now! Won't do drag without them! Emma, her partner, and her chihuahua welcomed us. We navigated around sewing machines, bolts of fabric, and streamers of trimming to a room that had foam squares waiting for us. "I'll be right back," Emma said, returning a moment later with markers, kitchen knives, and an electric knife. "Draw the shape of Africa. Then carve a mountain that peaks in the center of the top half. And smooth the edges so they blend nicely." North and West Africa become the ass cheek; Central, East and Southern Africa blend into the thigh after being compressed by layers and layers of tights.

I don't know what my drag would be without hip pads. The silhouette they produce changes my self-image. The way a sari drapes over them makes me feel . . . like a woman, womana, like my aunties, like an aunty. I barely knew Emma. I was only just getting to know Rhonda. But they both conspired to not only help my drag following the judges' critiques at *Drag Class*, but also gifted me a new way to see my body and to feel beautiful.

Aunties are known for their generosity, maybe to the point of excess. We are martyrs and will give it all away if we think you need it. So, you must accept our kindness, or else we'll take offense. As strange as it was to go to Emma's house to sit in a stranger's bedroom and take a carving knife to a piece of foam, it would have been too rude not to accept the welcome. It's a welcome that transformed my drag.

Being a drag aunty means opening your door to baby drag artists. Maya the Drag Queen met me at my mum's house in Bangalore to learn how to paint a cut crease on her eye makeup. I went to RuAfza's house in Medford to show them how to glue down thick desi eyebrows. Burhan learned to overdraw her lip chez moi. Scottie brought over a fluttering yellow cover-up when he came to visit knowing "those are your colors!" Kamani Sutra visited me in Boston so we could get ready together for her first public show. Lily carried, from New York to Boston, a box-load of designer heels that Fairy was disposing of to give to Kulfi Jaan. Anita sent me a box of wedding saris that she didn't want after her divorce. Nikita and Ish, clearing out deadstock from their Indian garment store, sent over bag-loads of blingy *lehengas* and *kurtis* for my drag children. At Berlin Nightclub in Chicago and Jacques Cabaret in Boston, I've attended drag wardrobe sales, where artists sell outfits they've rotated out of their repertoires for super cheap. This culture of gifting, lending, and bartering goods and services runs deep in drag communities.

Drag queens aunty each other through this culture of offerings: emotional support, career advice, performance planning, track-mixing, a couch to crash on, free clothes, and of course food.

Drag queens aunty each other through this culture of offerings. Emotional support, career advice, performance planning, track-mixing, a couch to crash on, free clothes, and of course food. Some of my favorite moments are post-show, when heels and corsets are off, but paint and wig caps are still on—just a bunch of weird gender freaks, huddled around not enough tater tots or whatever gross snack the bar is serving. Aunties feed each other both literally and figuratively. You can thank my drag aunties for these delicious hips!

TO AUNTY. THANKS FOR EVERYTHING. LAWHORE VAGISTAN.

In the drag world, we tend to fetishize drag mothers and fathers—borrowing from the language of normative western family structures as remixed by ball culture. Mothers and fathers opened doors and mentored us. They are the ones whose names we invoke when we describe our drag legacies. But drag is collective work, and *so many* people make and shape our drag! Talking about aunties is a chance to tell you about my drag aesthetics and style, but it also gives me the opportunity to bring to your attention the expansive network of generosity in drag communities, how drag artists aunty each other into the future.

I'm going to go ahead and assume you've seen *To Wong Foo, Thanks for Everything! Julie Newmar*. The film follows the adventures of three drag queens whose car breaks down in a small rural town, as they drive cross-country to compete in the *Miss Drag Queen of America* pageant. Two seasoned queens, Vida Boheme and Noxeema Jackson, agree to bring novice performer Chi-Chi Rodriguez with them on the ride. They refer to themselves as Aunty Vida and Auntie Noxee while doling out advice and explaining to Chi-Chi a taxonomy of transness and drag. You haven't seen it? Add it to your homework!

You'll remember that the impulsive Chi-Chi gets to flirt and flaunt, while Vida and Noxeema responsibly redecorate their temporary accommodations and give the women in town fabulous makeovers. Vida supports her host Carol-Ann as she endures an abusive relationship. Noxeema puts (trans)misogynists in their place with her blade-like nails. Beyond simply calling themselves aunties to Chi-Chi, they do the things aunties do: provide wisdom, style, space, and gossip. They aunty not only Chi-Chi but also the rest of the women in town, some even older than them, creating a cohort of women and queens who care for each other. It's exactly this cohort who comes to the drag queens' rescue at the end of the film.

Aunties aunty each other. They make room for other aunties' pleasure and freedom, and they tell other aunties how and how not to behave. Younger generations certainly feel the aunty effect the most. But when we don't acknowledge the dynamics of care and control between aunties, we're only seeing a partial picture.

[*IN ISABELLA ROSSELLINI VOICE*] NOW, A WARNING

Aunties are not easy. We are tired—if not exhausted. We've lived a lifetime of internalizing paltry honoraria, dropped gigs, dispersed protests, and sisters lost to transphobia. We've weathered racism, wars, fires in bars, shootings in nightclubs. Our bunions hurt. It's not a surprise, then, that aunty gossip sometimes turns sour, that aunty fashion can be slow to update itself, or that aunty's opinions take up a bit too much space. On behalf of myself and other drag aunties, I ask for your grace. Keep inviting us, and our drama, to the henna party. You have to admit, every party needs a little drama!

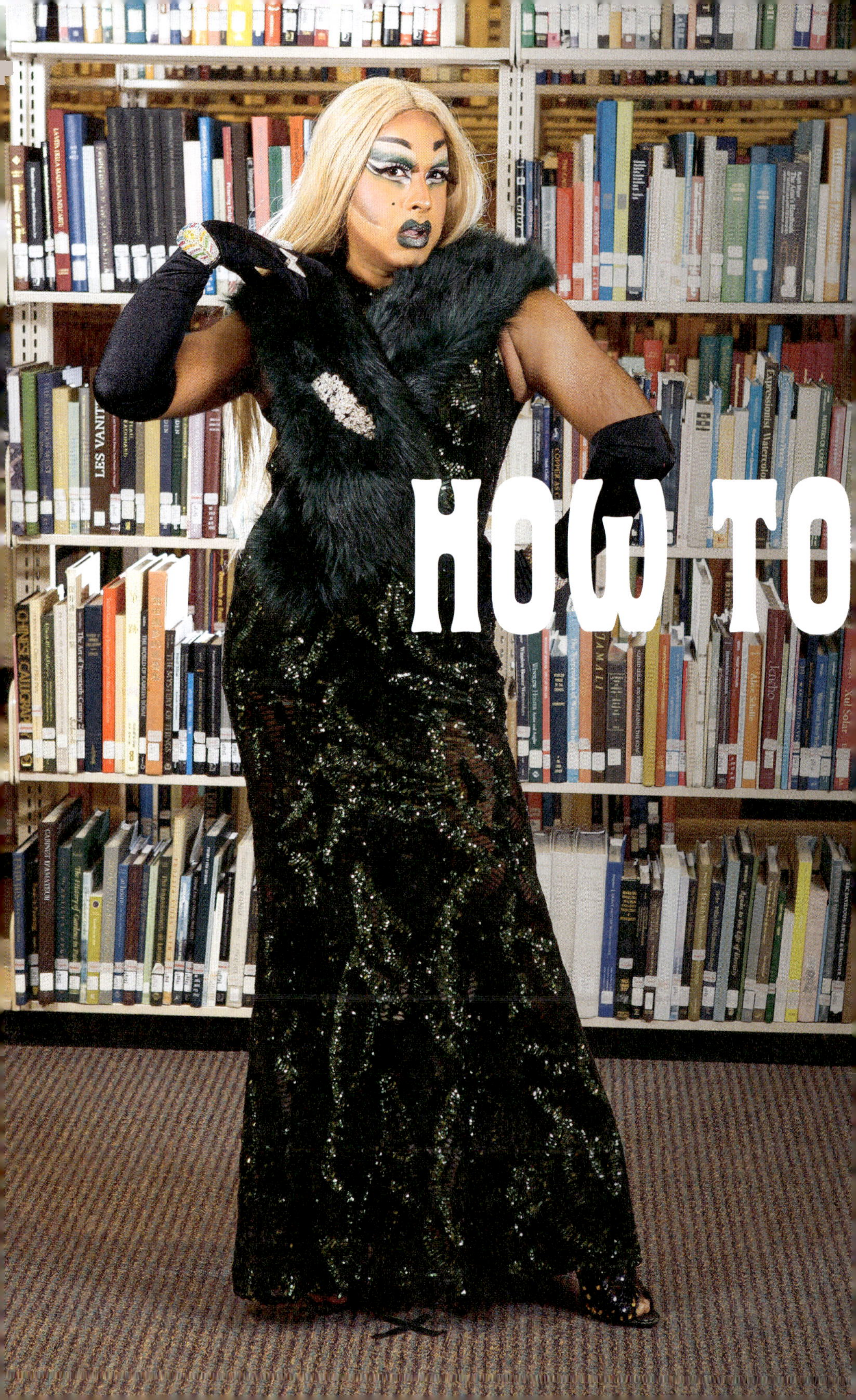

HOW TO

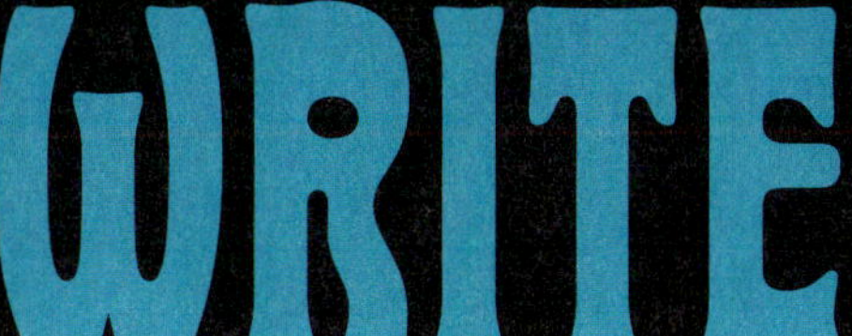

Aunty. Thank you for the chapter.
Excited to read
Will be a while till I get to it,
but will message when I've read.

so busy? on Sniffies?

No. OMG. Not Sniffies?
How do *you* know about that.
No, I have all this other writing.
Rec letters, peer reviews, tenure letters,
grant reports, grant submissions

wow. prolapse writer
*prolific (auto-correct)

It's all boring academic writing
Institutional bureaucratic formality

like all academic writing

Not necessarily!
I was actually thinking of
my next chapter being about writing

writing about writing 🧐

Writing about how
you have taught me to write
How to have ishtyle in my writing

i am mostly known
for my reading skills 👓📚

lol
Will send chapter when done.

💋

At a symposium in graduate school, I once prefaced my question to a senior South Asian gender and sexuality scholar with "Your outfit is phenomenal." A collective gasp consumed all the oxygen in the room and left me tripping over my words as I tried to ask a smart question about the relationship between photography and coloniality. I had committed a serious faux pas, drawing attention to the body of the scholar who had come to speak, that too a woman of color, instead of her mind, her brilliance, her ideas. But what I was trying to convey to her in my comment was my appreciation that she chose to deliver her brilliance, to give her paper, looking fierce as fuck. Black organza pussy bow under a gray suit. Hair cropped and faded, dyed a deep magenta. A mix of chunky and delicate silver jewelry. The curated image she made of herself suggested a preparedness to be there, to be seen *and* heard. Perfection. I wanted to be like her.

Bodies and bodily aesthetics have an impact on how we experience knowledge. I wanted to listen to that speaker, wanted to take in her exceptional ideas *because* she showed presence of self, choosing to bring herself into the room in a thought-out way that drew importance both to herself and her words. She staged her body as a conduit for her ideas, not an obstacle or inconvenience that needed to disappear itself. We pay very little attention to the aesthetics of public talks: pacing, eye contact, gesture, intonation. It frustrates me when the content is interesting but the delivery is dull. When the speaker doesn't look up from their paper; speaks in a monotone; forgets that there is even an audience present. Even scholars of performance forget that lecturing *is* performance and deliver the dryest talks. Egregious! The *Lessons in Drag* show reinvents the lecture, takes it to an extreme perhaps, but animates critical content *through* dress, movement, music, and audience interaction. It doesn't save the Q&A for the end of the talk, but keeps the audience engaged with three different opportunities for questions during the show. Performing as LaWhore has taught me how to bring artfulness to the lecture, but writing as LaWhore has also helped me to develop a style that addresses the reader as someone who is alive, and present, and has a body, and deserves to be engaged as such.

> Performing as LaWhore has taught me how to bring artfulness to the lecture, but writing as LaWhore has also helped me address the reader as someone who is alive, and present, and has a body.

Drag invites a certain kind of looking that is aesthetic as much as it is intellectual. How we deliver knowledge matters alongside what knowledge we present. Writing as LaWhore compels me to think about my writing style more broadly, to approach scholarly writing as a creative practice. As someone who didn't have a writing practice before graduate school, drag has offered me alternatives to the norms of academic expression.

WHY SO SERIOUS?

For those who aren't familiar with the ins and outs of academic publishing, most scholarly texts—including this book—go through a peer review process with multiple readers offering anonymous feedback on the manuscript. When I wrote *Ishtyle*, one of the reviewers made the astute and yet terrifying demand "LaWhore needs her own chapter. She is integral to this project." My response was to include a preface to the book titled "In Search of a Desi Drag Queen" that explained why drag wasn't the object of study, and that excused LaWhore from having to be so present in the book.

At that point, I didn't have the distance that I do now to reflect on my performance practice. I didn't have the confidence to take my own drag seriously as critical intellectual engagement. I was mired in the imposter syndrome that comes with being a junior scholar. I was even embarrassed to call myself a drag queen, because I only performed occasionally. But there was something very generous about that reviewer's request, their invitation to lean into and theorize the multiplicity I occupied in the field. But taking LaWhore seriously felt like unserious behavior, and she didn't get her due in *Ishtyle*. I tried to remedy this a little bit in *Decolonize Drag*, giving her the first and last word of the book. But why was it so difficult to be playful in my writing? Why couldn't I take LaWhore seriously? I had done it before.

The interview I published with LaWhore—the first "Lessons in Drag"—felt saucy and salacious to write. I felt like I was doing something self-indulgent, silly, and intentionally un-rigorous. I was just finishing graduate school and putting that piece together was like a palette cleanser. It was a much-needed chance to rehearse a different way of writing *just* after completing a colossal dissertation that was heavy with citation, argument, exposition—a text fighting to the death to be taken seriously.

My academic mentors always encouraged a rigorous practice of performative writing. Quick note: I'm using "performative" here not in the way it's used in popular culture to refer to practices that feel "fake," perfunctory acts without substantive intention. Within performance studies, we think of performative writing as that which acts on the reader, that leans into the fact that the reader and the author are active, embodied agents. It is writing that appeals to flesh, sensation, and movement. It looks like a lot of things: lush and descriptive; instructive, minimalist, and direct; confusing and choppy. It finds ways to interrupt mundane acts of reading and writing. My performance studies training gave me permission to be playful and strange.

Writing in LaWhore's voice was precisely the chance I needed to undermine the exhausting seriousness I had cultivated in myself.

So, the fact that I wrote my dissertation with the seriousness that I did was a result of *my own* self-consciousness, not any rigid requirements imposed on me by my grad school mentors. I had to convince myself of the urgency of queer nightlife as a site of political engagement. As I developed my dissertation chapters following my first round of fieldwork, I presented short papers at various conferences. At one of them, a musicologist came up to me after my talk and pronounced, "Your research sounds so *fun*." The way "fun" flicked off her lips made it feel like she had just called me a faggot. I love being a faggot, and I love that my research is fun. But instances like this sometimes make me retreat from fanciful faggoty writing. I feel forced to retreat to seriousness in order to legitimize fun.

Writing that interview was an opportunity to decompress from, and maybe even laugh at, the very form of academic writing I had so painstakingly practiced. Writing in LaWhore's voice was precisely the chance I needed to undermine the exhausting seriousness I had cultivated in myself.

I had never dreamed of being a drag queen. I had also never dreamed of being a writer. They both infiltrated my life around the same time. I did not have a "writing practice" prior to graduate school. I still don't. All the conventions I follow (or undermine) come from graduate school, from the peer review process, and from reading my colleagues' work. I write not for the love of language, but out of an investment in ideas and possibilities. I don't mean to suggest these are mutually exclusive. But when I'm not actively working on a book, article, or talk, writing isn't the medium I toy with or turn to in order to process the everyday. There are no literary fragments, incomplete scholarly projects, or even diaries hidden away in my apartment or hard drive the way there are half-mixed performance tracks, un-hemmed garments, and partially rhinestoned dresses.

I had never dreamed of being a drag queen. I had also never dreamed of being a writer. They both infiltrated my life around the same time.

I'm not a writer's writer. But LaWhore pushes me, nevertheless, to find artfulness in my writing, to reach beyond getting the point across to making choices about sentence length, word choice, and punctuation. Because I've had to develop her voice—one that feels appropriately casual and sassy when spoken aloud—I am forced to hone my own. This has been fun! It has not felt like I've compromised my academic integrity. To be honest, I'm tired of the slow pace of academic monographs. I *do* wish the sentences were shorter, chapters were fewer, and new terms the author tried to coin were less labored. I like where LaWhore is taking me.

CARTESIAN SPLITS

LaWhore and I experience the world differently. When I speak about her in the third person, when I write in her voice and then in mine, it's not because my ego is deeply fractured. I haven't done long-term Stanislavsky training to develop her persona. She's not a different person from me. But her audiences are much kinder to her than mine are to me. People want a photo with her. They want to tell her how stunning she is, not interrogate why she chose to use the term "feeling" instead of "affect." They tag *her* in Instagram posts about *Decolonize Drag* and not me. No one is out there questioning her for having "fun." Having her alongside me allows me to feel a set of feelings the academy doesn't immediately offer me access to. The way *she* moves through the world makes room for me to let go of insecurities.

But just as she shifts my self-perception, I think she also shifts yours. Writing in drag gives me permission to perform differently, because *you*, the reader, are primed to receive a drag queen in ways quite different from how you encounter an academic. Not all academic writing is as dry as the stereotypes would have it, but the genre does tend toward the sober.

In graduate school, my advisor responded to every observation I had about cultural phenomena with "So what?" Far from dismissive, this question required me to explain the social, historical, or intellectual circumstances in which my observations emerged, and explain how what I saw confirmed, diverted, refuted, built on, or confused what might be taken for granted. I learned how to make sure my reader understood why what I had to say mat-

Writing in drag gives me permission to perform differently, because *you*, the reader, are primed to receive a drag queen in ways quite different from how you encounter an academic.

tered. This vastly improved my scholarly writing. I'm not out here simply making observations in a vacuum, but instead situating them in a context—nothing I say falls out of a coconut tree.

But this kind of argumentative writing also conditions me to "insist" and "demonstrate" and "reveal." I'm working so hard to evidence my claims that I don't take the time to have fun. Moreover, because I write about fun things—drag, nightlife, fashion, camp, social dance, amateur theatre, aunties, food—I feel great pressure to "demonstrate" the urgency and seriousness of it all. My writing *has* to be framed as life-giving, if not life-saving!

Enter LaWhore. This bitch is under no obligation to make sense, let alone finish a thought. In her introduction to *Decolonize Drag* she offers a few observations about how drag colludes with and resists colonialism, capitalism, and carcerality, but then leaves it to me to do the work of historicization and explanation. I'm grateful for her. She gives me room to be a little bit more disaggregated than most types of scholarly writing allow. She interrupts me in our interviews with shade, song, and sympathy. In this way, she gives me a reason for mess and non-linearity. Crucially, though, the chaotic energy she brings to my writing always remains a tool to take care of the reader, rather than an excuse for self-indulgent erraticism.

Let me be clear: Not all performative writing is good. I often find that experimental writing in scholarly texts, while perhaps offering catharsis and pleasure for the writer, does not always take care of the reader. My experience with performative writing in critical scholarship has often been that it makes me do *more* work to understand an argument; it obscures the thesis rather than

> Writing *as* LaWhore has pushed me to make choices about how our voices differ. Writing in LaWhore's accent now forces me to encounter my own dominant accent, the default I tend to be oblivious to.

making it readily available. LaWhore does not write out of my self-indulgence, silliness, and subversion alone. She appears to offer the reader a kind assist, like the long-gone-but-not-forgotten Clippy in Microsoft Word.

Writing in multiple registers has been an opportunity for me to continue to undermine the rigor *expected* of academic writing, while also revealing *other* ways of staging deeply processed thought. Rigor, as Barbara Christian and José Esteban Muñoz have taught me, operates as an unspoken rubric for demonstrating expertise that specifically rewards knowledge about cis, white, straight, able-bodied, upper-caste, upper-class men. When fixed notions of scholarly "rigor" go uninterrogated and are left implicit, they devalue people of color's, women's, and queer people's experiences and knowledge systems.

Writing *as* LaWhore has pushed me to make choices about how our voices differ. This requires that I take a reflexive stance toward my writing style. When I write in the syntax that comes quickest to my fingers—scholarly argumentation geared toward humanities journals—I have to acknowledge that what I'm putting down on the page is *not* bad, just particular to that space. It's a style. Now the choice opens up of whether I want to conform to that style or not.

Why has it taken me so long to be able to articulate this? I mean, this is literally the argument of *Ishtyle*, that all styles *are* accented, not just minoritized ones. When we occupy dominant positions, we don't have to hear our own accent, so we don't have to acknowledge that the dominant mode is in fact *a mode*. Had I had the courage to take Reviewer No. 2's suggestion, I might have come to this realization way back when writing *Ishtyle*. I might have written a very different book. Writing in LaWhore's accent now forces me to encounter my own dominant accent, the default I tend to be oblivious to, and to decide if and how I want to reproduce it.

Learning to write in the academy produces a very particular *kind* of voice. Omise'eke Natasha Tinsley calls this her Beyoncé voice: the official, recognizable one. But she also writes her book *Ezili's Mirrors* through other Destiny's Child vocalists. Kelly is the voice of spirit knowledge, and Michelle speaks with Black feminist ancestors. They are differentiated by font, and every chapter features all three voices. It's comforting to know that I'm not the only one who is both comfortable with my academic voice and its legibility, and also aware that it could benefit from accompaniment.

Beyond leading me to an awareness of my dominant writing voice, LaWhore also helps me work through my ideas in a methodical way. When she asks me questions, she expects an answer. When scholars in the humanities and social sciences write, we sometimes include a driving question or a list of questions that have shaped the project. I'm sure you've seen that paragraph-long list of questions that follows an essay's thesis statement. This tendency feels like a relic of the early 2000s, though it's still going strong today. These questions are usually rhetorical devices, possibly answered *somewhere* in the essay, but mostly introduced early on to open up a conversation. But in the interview format, LaWhore places pressure on me to answer questions directly, right away. She's sometimes quite mean about it and doesn't let me meander.

The advantages of this became clear to me when I read bell hooks's interview with Gloria Watkins—that is, herself. In her landmark book *Teaching to Transgress*, hooks explores her relationship to the work of Brazilian philosopher Paulo Freire by interviewing herself. This allows her to introduce a first-person perspective in her analysis of Freire's ideas, combining her summary of his work with an account of how it has impacted her. Watkins places pressure on hooks: "be more specific"; "so you see no contradiction . . . ?" Watkins makes hooks's thinking spicy. She forces her to sharpen her argument. Even the illustrious Nicki Minaj interviews herself, Nicole and Nicki in conversation for *Elle* in 2012. This interview, Uri McMillan argues, provides Nicki the opportunity to set up questions that allow her to "subversively respond to critics in creative and unexpected ways."

E. Patrick Johnson also uses the interview format beautifully when he fictionalizes both himself (as Dr. EPJ) and his research discoveries (as Miss B) in his book *Honeypot*. With Dr. EPJ, Johnson stages himself as a naïve interlocutor. This allows Miss B to educate both him *and* the reader about Black queer women's lives. This ruse allows the audience to experience the unfurling of data, analysis, and theory, as Dr. EPJ learns *from* Miss B and the women she introduces him to. So rather than an academic analysis in which Johnson is the expert theorist of Black women's lives who has already completed all the intellectual work before writing the book, Miss B and Dr. EPJ's interaction shows how scholarship actually stews and brews through dialogue and process.

Including LaWhore in *Decolonize Drag* was not only a playful device to clue the reader into the themes of the book. I wanted to signal to my reader that, even as a scholar and a critic, I have an investment in the *doing* of drag. LaWhore's contribution to *Decolonize Drag* insists on the book's material stakes. The things I write about drag are not simply the grand—though well-researched—opinions of an ivory-towered scholar. The critiques, compliments, and hopes I express have very tangible consequences for how LaWhore and I operate in the world. People forget this when they read scholarly work. Scholars—especially queer and trans scholars, people of color, first-generation folks, disabled people—research and write for our own survival and world-making, and not simply to pander to the institution.

Some scholars research and write for our own survival and world-making, and not simply to pander to the institution. Having that not-me who can write *with me* allows me to insert myself into my research in a way that lets readers know that I have a major stake in what I'm saying—but at the same time am not about to subject them to relentless na-

Some scholars research and write for our own survival and world-making, and not simply to pander to the institution.

vel-gazing autoethnography. Narrating my own work through and as a drag queen allows audiences to conjure flesh, body, dress in a way that they don't usually do for an author. We often tuck the author's photo away on the back page, trying not to color the reader's impression of the text with the body of the writer. Not LaWhore. She demanded to be the first image in *Decolonize Drag*. Writing in drag insists that a body was involved, that chunky rings and beaded bracelets made the writing process more cumbersome. Have *you* ever tried typing with acrylics on?

> Drag insists that my writing remember that there are bodies on both sides of the text: writer *and* reader. Why not write with people in mind who are just as fleshy, desirous, and perplexed as me?

DRAG YOURSELF!

LaWhore has taught me how to look at my own scholarship, scholarly voice, and intellectual training from a critical distance. LaWhore's brazen confidence offers me and my readers an ease and flow that soothes the paranoid voice of the critical scholar. At no point, though, do I want my reader's takeaway to be "academic writing bad; drag writing good." Scholarly writing is its own craft. At its best, it is an elegant practice of escorting a reader through the anatomy of a social, material, aesthetic, or theoretical problem. Given the horrifyingly violent world we live in—in which multiple systemic forces control our bodily autonomy, curtail our participation in the political sphere, exterminate whole populations, and wreak havoc on the planet—intricate writing is necessary to explain the complexity of our condition. Good scholarly prose can patiently teach us unwieldy ideas.

Where I think drag has stepped in to help me is in insisting my writing remember that there are bodies on both sides of the text. The writer *and* the reader. So why not write with *people* in mind? Moreover, why not write with people in mind who are just as fleshy, desirous, and perplexed as me? Why not appeal to the senses through font size and text placement and images, alongside luscious language and the magnificent minimalism of good theory?

I mean it when I say LaWhore experiences the world differently from me. People are kinder to her, more welcoming and open, more flirtatious and intrigued. Sure, she is disruptive, but in a delightful way. So, as I write, and maybe as you read, why not lean into the delight?

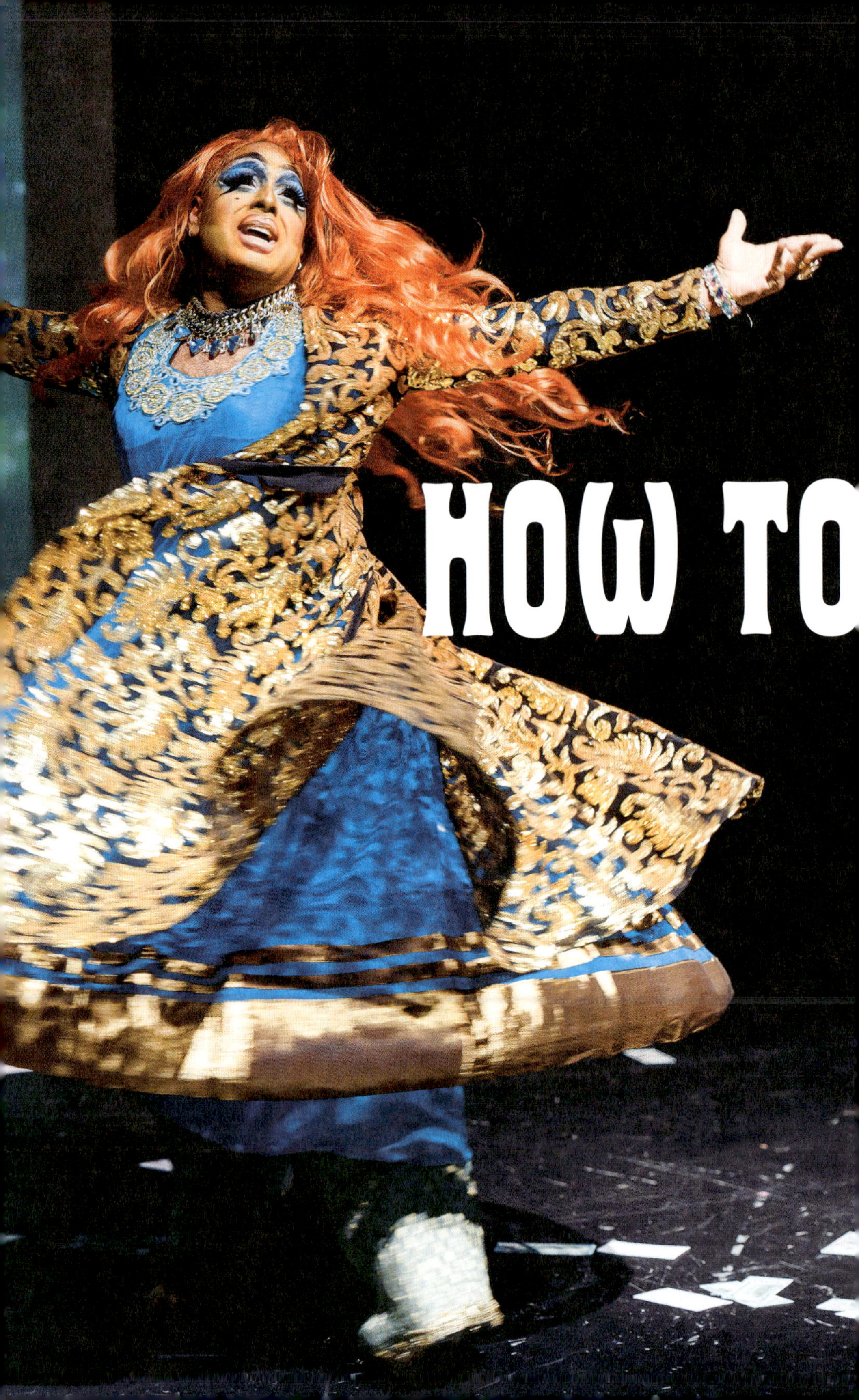

HOW TO

BE A MAP

so now everyone knows
we're the same person

I think that's been obvious for a while?
Brandeis University Press's readership
is pretty smart, no?

then this is so cringe.
yr literally typing a text message
w/ yourself

Yes. But I feel like I've argued
why that's valuable . . . ?

Yes. tell yourself that

At the end of the day, I rely on you
to do a lot of work for me
It's not a secret or surprise
It's a lot of intellectual work

plus emotional labor

Emotional labor?

Pls. don't pretend professor trying to compress yr whole migration story into me

I haven't the faintest idea what you mean LaWhore 😶 But feel free to read me for filth

I was birthed in a break. I live as Kareem's desire for a different geography: a subcontinent unfractured by colonialism, a diaspora formed of desire and not displacement, an unsettled map that traverses diasporas and subcontinent. How to embody his queer cartography? How do I *be* Vagistan?

He makes a big ask. But I have a big ego. I am up for the challenge. Like all good whores, I begin on my knees.

I begin on my knees. Barefoot. Do you understand what it's like to be barefoot as a drag queen? You lose all your cunty power. Those heels aren't holding your ass high anymore. The stockings over my feet make me look like a web-footed goose. I feel naked, despite the black net robe shimmering with gold sequin motifs swallowing my body. The robe covers me from neck to floor, and spreads in a circle around me. On the projector behind me, white-gray smoke spirals onto the screen. Jyoti Nooran starts to vocalize, and the emotions swell out of her throat, echoing as wide as an empty canyon. I lip-synch her melancholic melody, eyes closed as news clips sound over her voice.

I live as Kareem's desire for a different geography. How do I *be* Vagistan?

. . . must make very clear this is not a Muslim ban. It's not a travel ban. It's a vetting system to keep America safe. That's it . . .

Sewan Sharif mein Hazrat Laal Shahbaaz Qalandar ki dargaah ke haathe mein dhamaake ke ittilaat hain, aur muttaadid afraad ke zakhmi hone ki bhi ittila mil rahi hai. Breaking news aapko de rahe hain . . .

Engineer Srinivas Kuchibotla was killed and another Indian man and an American were injured after a Navy veteran yelling "get out of my country" and "terrorist" opened fire . . .

Gunmen walked into a Sikh temple in Oak Creek, Wisconsin, and opened fire . . .

Six people have been killed in a shooting at a mosque in Quebec city . . .

2015, an angry mob in India beat a Muslim man to death over accusations that he had eaten . . .

Gujarat's Puna. Four Dalit men were stripped and flogged by gau rakshas for allegedly skinning a dead cow . . .

These attacks targeting the Muslim community in Christchurch as they happen during Friday prayers inside the mosque . . .

As one of the first Muslim women to serve in Congress, Democrat Ilhan Omar says she has faced increased death threats . . .

There is fear and mistrust of opposition leader Narendra Modi and his right-wing Hindu nationalist BJP party . . .

In March 2017, I was scheduled to perform at a queer South Asian drag night called *Adaa* at Machine Nightclub in Boston. The months leading up to this gathering were awful. Donald Trump had recently been inaugurated into the US presidency. His election should not have been a surprise—white supremacy, misogyny, empire-making, and capitalism are core to this country. He immediately effected Order 13769, which we fondly call "the Muslim ban." I was dreading this performance. What would it mean to gather, in the club, in the wake of such public calamity? Everybody was depressed for the many reasons noted in the news clips I had spliced together: xenophobia that led to a Hindu Indian immigrant's murder; US, Canadian, Pakistani, and New Zealand Islamophobia that led to attacks on Muslim, Sufi, and Sikh spaces; US anti-Blackness, misogyny, and Islamophobia that made Ilhan Omar a perpetual target; Indian Brahminical supremacy that led to the lynching of Dalits and Muslims.

What was I supposed to perform for a community that had spent the previous months protesting, or else laying low, worrying about visa renewals and loved ones stranded abroad?

I kind of hoped the show would be canceled. But it wasn't. Queer nightclub spaces are few in Boston and quickly disappearing—eight years later, Machine is now a high-rise condo building. If we canceled this show, we probably couldn't host something else for a long time. The night had been scheduled for months, and the community deserved a little bit of fun. In fact, in anticipation of the show, a group of queer desis visited me at home for a little lesson in drag, in which I walked them through the fundamentals of makeup and performance. The girlies were ready! But in this moment, performing for a queer South Asian audience, I couldn't just do a sensual Helen number, a slutty Raveena bop. Oh the pressure!

I ended up creating a performance that mixed three versions of the song "Damadam Mast Qalandar," a praise song for Sufi saint Lal Shahbaz Qalandar, spliced with news clips and voiceovers from prominent public figures, as quoted above. For those not familiar with this *iconic* song, let Aunty educate you. "Damadam" is a qawwali, a song style from the courts of the fourteenth-century Delhi sultanate. Qawwali music praises Sufi saints and other spiritual figures, using the language of rapture, love, and intoxication. I continue to use this number in the *Lessons in Drag* show when explaining drag's responsibility to engage with and respond to the legacies of history in the present. That was the performance in which I felt, for the first time, like Vagistan. Interestingly, it was by embodying *sound*—in prose, poetry, vocalization, and instrumentation—that I was able to hold the many messy places of Dr. Khubchandani's itinerary together, for a little while. Researching this performance pushed me to invest more deeply in being Vagistan, becoming that place for him, and for others for whom geography has to be worn because there is no physical place to be at home.

Early on in the *Lessons in Drag* show, before I get to "Damadam Mast Qalandar," I do a whole bit about where the name LaWhore Vagistan comes from. "LaWhore because my family originates from what is now Pakistan. Lahore but with a W. Because I'm here to *werq*." I even have a slide that shows typically female anatomy layered over the subcontinent, a cartography that is "more capacious, that extends beyond its limits, that reaches into regions often not included in the vision of South Asia. Sexual and pleasurable!" Together, the words and visuals try to capture a sexual excess and abundance, something beyond the heteronormative reproduction that is always tied to statehood. But sometimes it doesn't feel like enough. Or it feels too conceptual to actually put on my body.

Let's get academic for a second. In developing his theory of "the aural border," Josh Kun reconsiders geographies "as a field of sound, a terrain of musicality and music-making, of static and noise, of melodic convergence and dissonant clashing . . . opening the doors to a new archive of historicity and analysis, a new methodology of understanding the audio formation of national and social identities within specific, delineated geopolitical territories." What does this even mean? To me, he's saying that music and sound are often bound to the places they emerge from. For that reason, sound offers an opportunity for places that are often bordered off from each other physically and even ideologically, policed and

By embodying *sound*—in prose, poetry, vocalization, and instrumentation—I could hold the many messy places of Dr. Khubchandani's itinerary together.

kept apart in sometimes violent ways, to meet, match, and manifest something together.

Carefully curating the soundscape for the *Adaa* performance was the closest I've come to assembling the various geographies that matter to Dr. Khubchandani's history, politics, and desires. The closest I've come to Vagistan.

QAWWALI AT THE RAMROD

Soon after I moved to Boston, in the fall of 2016, the organizers of MASALA Boston asked, "LaWhore, would you host a drag workshop at your home? We're excited that you've moved here and want to learn from you." MASALA is the Massachusetts Area South Asian Lambda Association; the effort that went into that acronym is unparalleled! MASALA emerged alongside Trikone-Bay Area, SALGA in New York, Sangat in Chicago, and Khush in DC. These organizations have always understood that music and dance are integral to relieving the alienation queer migrants experience, and have hosted nightlife events like *Kulture Kulcha* and *Color Me Queer*.

The MASALA Boston drag workshop gave local queers a little confidence to perform, my new drag babies! We decided to do a show on March 25, 2017, at the appropriately named Ramrod, the upstairs bar of Machine Nightclub. But what to perform following the dumpster fire of the 2016 election? So many in our South Asian community were thrown into disarray by the Muslim bans issued in the weeks prior. How to celebrate, be irreverent, feel beautiful, and enjoy each other's company in the shadow of a fascist and virulently Islamophobic administration? *Adaa* was certainly about pleasure and fun, but for the brown queers gathering that night, we

How to celebrate, be irreverent, feel beautiful, and enjoy each other's company in the shadow of a fascist, virulently Islamophobic administration?

didn't have the luxury of forgetting that our collectivity made us more abject, more threatening, more like each other.

I thought about performing "Damadam Mast Qalandar," but did it belong at the Ramrod?

Jyoti Nooran falls into silence as the news clips fade out. Then a summoning voice bursts out of her silence.

Ho laal meri pat,
rakhiyon bala jhoole laalan

My eyes have opened, and I lip synch,
gesturing directly at the audience.

Sindhri da, Sehwan da

My hands gesture this way, then that.

Sakhi shabaaz qalandar
Damadam mast qalandar

Her sister Sultana responds:

Damadam mast qalandar

The audience immediately takes
my cue and starts clapping.
The pace has quickened.

Ali har harde andar
Sultana: *Ali har harde andar*
Ali da pehla number
Sultana: *Ali da pehla number*
Ho lal meri, ho lal meri.

"Damadam Mast Qalandar" praises Sindhi deity Jhulelal, Sufi saint Lal Shahbaz Qalandar, and Muslim eminence Hazrat Ali. The singer calls to the red-robed saint for protection, the saint who watches over both Sindh and Sehwan. The singer devotes their ecstatic breaths to the saint. The singer lights lamps in honor of the saint. Its lyrics were composed by thirteenth- and eighteenth-century Sufi poets, and in particular the daddy of qawwali, Amir Khusrow. Its current melody was set for a Pakistani film in the 1950s, but it was Bangladeshi playback singer Runa Laila's 1970s version that really blew up. I associate "Damadam Mast Qalandar" most intimately with my Sindhi aunties, most of whom were transplants to Ghana, migrating to marry merchants—it's always the women who have to move. It's a song they would take any opportunity to sing, summoning others to join them, at weddings, Diwali celebrations, and temple activities.

On Christmas Eve, 2016, I was at Le Poisson Rouge in New York watching my drag sister Lal Batti dance at DJ Rekha's *Bollywood Disco* night. Rekha started spinning a 2014 version of "Damadam Mast Qalandar" sung by Yo Yo Honey Singh and Mika Singh. Lal and I immediately dropped our gossip session and started to spin. This iteration of the song has a heavy bass element that was perfect for the nightclub. It felt shocking and irreverent to dance to it there, with another drag queen, with a queer DJ clapping us on as we twirled and over-exaggeratedly lip-synched the song as a hymn of praise and flirtation to each other's queer divinity. On stage with Rekha and Lal, this song, even when sung by bhangra bros, became ecstatically queer.

When strange sounds arrive in the nightclub, they have the capacity to repair the chasms keeping apart our beauty, our spirituality, our homes, our erotic desires, our families, our bodies. Sound offers them a border to meet again. I had so much fun dancing to this song that night and it stayed on my mind as a possible drag number.

On February 16, 2017, the shrine of Sufi saint Lal Shahbaz Qalandar—the figure venerated in the song—was attacked by an ISIS-affiliated suicide bomber who killed more than eighty people. "Damadam Mast Qalandar," which actually names Sehwan, the site of his shrine, accumulated even more intensity. I had to perform it. I wanted to address the Muslim ban and also the attack on the shrine. I wanted to acknowledge the multi-sited violence that makes minoritarian life precarious.

MANY MAST QALANDARS

But what version to perform? The Bollywood bro version didn't seem quite right—not my aunty aesthetic, you know. But I didn't want to completely do away with the nightclub feel. How to hold the gravity and multiplicity of this song and its many contexts, to dance it for Sehwan and South Asian diasporas at the same time?

There's this version I really like, from an Indian reality TV competition called *Sur Kshetra*; Atif Aslam leads the Pakistani team and Himesh Reshammiya leads the Indian team. In one episode, a contestant doesn't perform "Damadam Mast Qalandar" to the judges' satisfaction. And so the show's hosts invite Runa Laila, who is on the judges' panel, to show her how it's done. You think it's just going to be Runa doing her same old expert thing she always does, but then Abida Parveen, who is also a judge, starts singing "Ali Ali Ali Ali, Maula Maula," and then Asha Bhosle adds her mellifluous "Aaaaaaaaaaaa." Out of I-don't-know-where, Atif Aslam joins in, harmonizing the main melody with "Ghanan Ghanan Teri Naubat Baje," and I want to fall out of my chair. And the best part of all of it is that Himesh Reshammiya simply sits still, knowing not to interfere. I don't know if this was planned for that episode or if the spirit simply carried all four singers into ecstasy, but it is one of my favorite things in the media universe. Icons of India, Pakistan, and Bangladesh, singing together across genre, language, religion, dress style, and gender presentation.

In the video, Abida performs an exciting androgyny, using neutral colors and cuts in her clothing. Abida describes herself as an ant, as opposed to a man or a woman—minuscule in the face of God. Runa Laila, the person who popularized the song so widely, is also a key figure in founding South Asian disco, especially in her collaborations with Bappi Lahiri. Although you'll often imagine her in a respectable sari, hair in an aunty bouffant, one of her first albums was called *Super Runa* and had her in a Wonder Woman-esque outfit on the cover. And Asha has been key to shaping Indian femininity through her voice, particularly in contrast to her sister Lata Mangeshkar's. Asha and Lata come from a lineage of courtesans, repurposing that artistic tradition as pre-eminent playback singers in the Hindi film industry. Lata always voiced the innocent, virginal heroines, while Asha sang the sultrier songs for the vamps and vixens. There's just so much fucking gender happening in this clip.

> **When strange sounds arrive in the nightclub, they make a messier map for us.**

You know, when diasporic drag queens feel like we have to perform something like Kesha's "Praying," rather than a qawwali like this, to manifest mourning, hope, desire, and devotion in the nightclub, we are making a compromise. We lose the other feelings, meanings, and aesthetics of gender that are attached to our many elsewheres, the many embodiments of our own chaotic divas. We need sound to make a messier map for us.

This track, the "Damadam Mast Qalandar" from *Sur Kshetra,* felt like Vagistan, like the hopeful reimagining of borders, faiths, and histories. But I also had to be realistic. The song is perfect. But playing four people at once wouldn't make for a good lip synch. I let that one go. I'm talented but not that talented.

I did love that this version had icons of Bangladesh, India, and Pakistan singing together. I allowed that to lead me, and made a medley that I think captures some of its magic. First up are the Nooran Sisters performing live in Dhaka. The Nooran Sisters track is an interesting one to perform to. Jyoti initiates the line and Sultana follows, a call and response. When I perform it, I only do Jyoti's part. Her voice is *so* powerful. In fact, a small clip of this track went viral on TikTok and Instagram; the meme has people jumping in fear and scattering at the forceful sound of her voice as it bursts through her body. When Sultana responds, she gives the audience a clue of what to do. I love when I have South Asians in the audience—they know exactly *how* to respond. They sing Sultana's part with her!

During this lip synch, I'm on my knees, in a single spotlight. The projection fills with visuals of smoke, as if incense is pouring into the space. I'm swinging my head and twisting my wrists to capture the force of Jyoti's sound. Without fail, as I move from the slow vocalization to the rhythmic outbursts, the audience begins to clap along, as if they've been anticipating, needing, this catharsis from the sudden seriousness of the show.

Jyoti Nooran closes the verse out. I get up from the pool of light that has me glowing in the darkened space. Linda Sarsour begins to speak:

> I am every Islamophobe's worst nightmare as a woman who is Muslim, and empowered, and loud, and proud, and from Brooklyn, and Palestinian, and I wear a hijab, and I run my mouth, and I'm on national television, and I'm hanging out with you.

Going from the Nooran Sisters into Linda Sarsour's commentary helps you feel the musicality of Linda's voice. I enumerate each of the social categories she lists on my fingers. Her ten-part self-description bangs out its own kind of rhythm. It doesn't feel jarring paired with the song. When she's done, I snap my fingers and turn my back to the audience in a fierce huff. Linda's name appears on the screen. Audiences should know that when I'm lip-synching about being Palestinian, Muslim, wearing a hijab, that I'm embodying *someone else*. The I that's speaking is clearly not *me*. For this section, I'm back on my feet, sassy in the beginning and then more and more earnest as she keeps going.

Sarsour's voice returns:

> Muslims are about 1.8 billion people in the world. We are the fastest-growing religion. And when you take the actions of a few and you paint with a broad brush a whole entire community you are alienating 1.8 billion people in the world. So i-i-i-it's really sad that every time there's a terrorist attack that Muslims hold their heart and say "please god don't let be a Muslim," because people know the backlash that comes with that. Because not only are we horrified by the actual act that happens, but then we have to worry about the retaliation that some of our fellow Americans, and oftentimes the government, with their policies, engage against Mu-M-Muslim communities, that have nothing to do with these terrorist attacks.

When I have to lip-synch this brilliant and experienced orator stumbling over her words, it reveals to the audience how *difficult* it is for Linda to make sense of the horror of the situation. Lip-synch makes apparent the labor behind speech, and to see the difficulty it takes to find language in times of terror.

Tipping has a very important role in drag, especially US drag. Accepting tips gives us a reason to go up to our audience, to interact, to touch, to share some kind of intimacy.

TOUCHING, FEELING

Audiences never tip during "Damadam Mast Qalandar." It isn't flashy and feel-good. But tipping has a very important role in drag, especially US drag. Yes, of course, it allows performers to make a little bit more money than the paltry sum the venue or the organizers pay us for the gig. But the practice of accepting tips also gives us a reason to go up to our audience, to interact, to touch, to share some kind of intimacy. At this point in the performance, I have been alone on stage belting some of the most intense material in the show so far. I feel alone. The audience probably feels tense. And we need to remember that we are there in the space together.

Komal Rizvi sings "Damadam Mast Qalandar" now. This is her version from Pakistan's Coke Studio, accompanied by Balochi folk singer Akhtar Chanal Zahri. Her voice is calming and her pace is slow.

Ho laal meri,

I start to walk toward the audience.

Oh laal meri,

And reach out for a hand. We hold; we squeeze; we let go.

Ho laal meri pat,

Repeat. And repeat. And repeat.

Rakhiyon bala jhoole laalan

Repeat, until the verse runs out.

Touching the audience, having a moment of flesh-to-flesh contact, feels like a relief. I'm tired at this point. I've been doing all this work for everyone else. It's nice just to be reminded I am there in the flesh with other people. At college shows, I can anticipate the excitement of baby brown queers hoping I will come and hold their hands. Their palms are sweaty with the opportunity to encounter "an elder," perhaps even practice a kind of reciprocal intergenerational care by assuring me they are there with me. Occasionally, there are white men in the audience, jocks, legs splayed, slumped low in their seats, required to be there by their professors. They extend their hands to me because they were taught good manners.

Sindhri da, Sehwan da

I gesture to Sindh and to Sehwan.

Sakhi shabaaz qalandar

As her voice rises in triumph, I run back to the stage, holding up my gold and black robe to keep from tripping.

Damadam mast qalandar

Hips, breasts, and head pulse.

Ali da pehla number

Sexy and sultry.

Sakhi shabaaz qalandar

Playful and fetching.

Ho laj meri, ho laj meri.
Hind Sindh peera peera
teri nau hat vaaje

Akhtar Chanal Zahri interjects, a twanging instrument giving more vibrance to his voice.

Ali da pehla number
Ali dum dum be andar

Hips and tits and shoulders and neck.
I am all jhatkas and thumkas.
Komal Rizvi steps back in.

Hind Sindh peera teri nau bat vaaje
Naal baje ghadi yaal bala jhoole laalan
Sindhri da, Sehwan da
Sakhi shabaz qalandar
Damadam mast qalandar
Sakhi shabaz qalandar.

The track includes the voice of a Baloch singer alongside the distinct sound of his regional string instruments. This "rustic" sound of Balochi masculinity beautifully ruffles the ethereality of Sufi voice. During this part of the track, I let go of the qawwali-style gestures, and instead serve folksy *thumkas, jhatkas,* and *matkas.* I shake my hips and bust and shoulders in ways that feel flirtatious and sexy. As much as this performance was—and still is—about the gravity of our political context, it is impossible for me not to summon the way my aunties dance to this song. I'm always amazed by how sexy their performances feel when I recreate them. When I watched them perform for each other—I spent hundreds of afternoons in my faggy childhood watching them rehearse dances together—they made movement and song for each others' pleasure.

One of my most recent encounters with "Damadam Mast Qalandar" was at a 2019 wedding in New Jersey. Aunty Sharmila's son was getting married, and the families were hosting the Sangeet, a night of song and dance. At the end of the night, after the DJ was done and the lights had come on, Aunty Sharmila's group of friends from Ghana gathered around to sing for her. Their song wasn't for the bride and groom; it didn't happen during the party itself. It was a little bit of stolen time, a moment for the Sindhi aunties to enjoy the night and feel fun and fabulous and familiar.

Mika Singh sings:

Damadam mast qalandar

My mixing is perfect and the transition from Komal Rizvi's folksy version to this Bollywoodized club thumper is seamless. It's the one that DJ Rekha spun, but it feels different after what we've just gone through together.

Ah mast e dil de andar

I pull at the sash that has been holding the sequin coat closed.

Ali da pehla number

The coat falls open, and the *kalis* of my copper-trimmed turquoise Anarkali unfurl, finally having room to blossom.

Sakhi shabaz qalandar

I bring my hands below my sternum, in a kathak dancer's resting position.

Oh laal meri, oh laal meri

Yo Yo Honey Singh raps:

Mera yaar vi tu

Chakkar [spin].

Mera pyaar vi tu

Chakkar.

Meri jeet vi tu

Chakkar.

Meri haar vi tu

Chakkar.

Mera dil da ai

The coat fans out and the sequins catch the light with each spin.

Dildar vi tu

The Anarkali blooms wide and the fills the space with turquoise and copper sparkle.

Mera zindagi pe

Each turn allows the costume
to pulsate.

Aitbaar vi tu

A glittering heartbeat.

Mera momin tu

And I spin.

Mera qaazi tu

And spin.

Mera ruseya tu

And spin.

Mera raazi tu

And spin.

Mera aab vi tu

My body has exploded

Mera aatish tu

Into a disco ball

Mera dushman tu

As sequins

Mera aashiq tu

And mirrors

Mera din vi tu

And trimmings

Meri raat vi tu

Catch the light

Meri rooh vi tu

And I'm dizzy

Meri zaat vi tu

And the room is spinning

Main ton door vi tu

And if I don't stop

Mere saath vi tu

I will fall.

Iss kaafir di

I can't see the audience anymore.

Auqaat vi tu

I fall to my knees.

Allah hoo.

And the coat keeps spinning, wrapping itself around me. I feel safe inside of it.

For the final part of the medley, I don't lip-synch. I let the bhangra bros lead us into the club. Instead I turn. And turn. And turn. Beginning first with wobbly chakkars I remember from my few months of kathak training, pivoting on the heel and spotting myself in order to complete the turn. But then I launch into faster turns, unregulated by repertoire, childlike, losing my sense of space, balance, and self. These turns, familiar from many kinds of Sufi performance and other forms of social, ritual, and concert dance, launch my sequin coat into the air. When the spinning sequins catch the light, they create an ethereal luminescence!

After watching me perform this number, a colleague at Brandeis offered gratitude for the vulnerability I had shown. He said that seeing me perform, eyes closed, during the Nooran Sisters part of the number, disappearing into myself, felt intimate to him. He said it was so rare to see such interiority on stage. I decided to be sassy and burst his bubble, telling him that those moments in which my eyes were closed were in fact the most contrived. A good drag performer knows her *abhinaya*, knows that her audience accesses her through her eyes, and makes choices about when to close them, to perform that "going inward." But I'm not that much of a bitch, and did offer something of myself. I admitted that the most vulnerable moment was actually at the end of the number, when I spun and spun till my mind gave up all intention, and my coat burst into a disco ball, and the club lights became a galaxy, and the audience suddenly felt like it was all around me, and I truly gave up control.

If you're used to watching drag shows, you'll know that the pop song format shapes the arc of the performance: verse, chorus, verse, chorus, bridge, verse, chorus / outro. A clean three-and-a-half-minute number. The repetitive structures of devotional songs do something different to the performance and the performer. Sufi music shifts drag's linear sense of time and space. Time for a citation again. In his study of devotional practices at and around the shrine of Lal Shahbaz Qalandar, Omar Kasmani theorizes what he calls the "un-straight" affordances and affective intimacies that Sufism offers. These affordances are grounded not simply in imagined and felt relationship to the saint, but also in the material conditions that govern the shrine, the city, and the bodies that move through them both.

The repetitive structures of devotional songs do something different to the performance and the performer. Sufi music shifts drag's linear sense of time and space.

Sufi music has been co-opted into nationalist projects by Pakistani media and secularized by Bollywood cinema. However, Arshia Haq, founder of the club night *Discostan*, uses this genre in diasporic nightclub spaces to blur national distinctions and invite dancers into ecstatic collectivity. The Sufi sounds she spins aren't always the slick mixes coming out of Bollywood or Coke Studio, but sometimes recordings from her travels to the shrine of Lal Shahbaz Qalandar, tracks that might last for more than ten minutes, offering up a kind of repetition that spins revelers into a *haal* or trance.

Giving myself up to the track, taking its permission to indulge in repetition, I too give of myself to the audience. I let performance take over!

The performance I made for *Adaa*, and that I continue to perform in *Lessons in Drag*, is in many ways stuck in 2017, the moment of the

Muslim ban. But it is a performance that feels helpful to return to, not only because the xenophobic violence it critiques continues to replay in the rise of white supremacist fascism in the US and in the territorial wars impinging on and around Kashmir, but because it productively disorganizes my highly controlled drag practice. It returns me to my aunties, their bodies, their pleasures. It takes me beyond myself, requires me to pause and catch my breath and steady my vision in order to keep performing.

My "Damadam Mast Qalandar" number is certainly not perfect, and it transforms with audience, location, lighting, becoming something new each time. Since October 2023, I've edited the projected backdrop at the end to include a shower of watermelons and the text "Free Palestine" to protest the ongoing genocide in Palestine. This feels urgent, especially given my use of Linda Sarsour's 2017 speech, to highlight how Palestinian feminist critique remains critical to ongoing struggles for justice and liberation.

This performance, like a map, conjures spatial relations. For many displaced populations, including diasporic Hindu Sindhis like myself, loss is central to our individual and shared narratives. If we're not careful, loss becomes our only narrative. Repeating this performance reminds me that I am constantly learning from Palestinians—from diasporic artists and activists, from those surviving occupation in Gaza and the West Bank—that under conditions of loss, there are still resources to build abundant worlds.

The promiscuous itinerary of this song, the abundance, repetition, and multiplicity it affords, makes new kinds of place by reorganizing borders, genders, affects, and aesthetics. Letting this multiplicity take over my body, I become Vagistan.

HOW TO

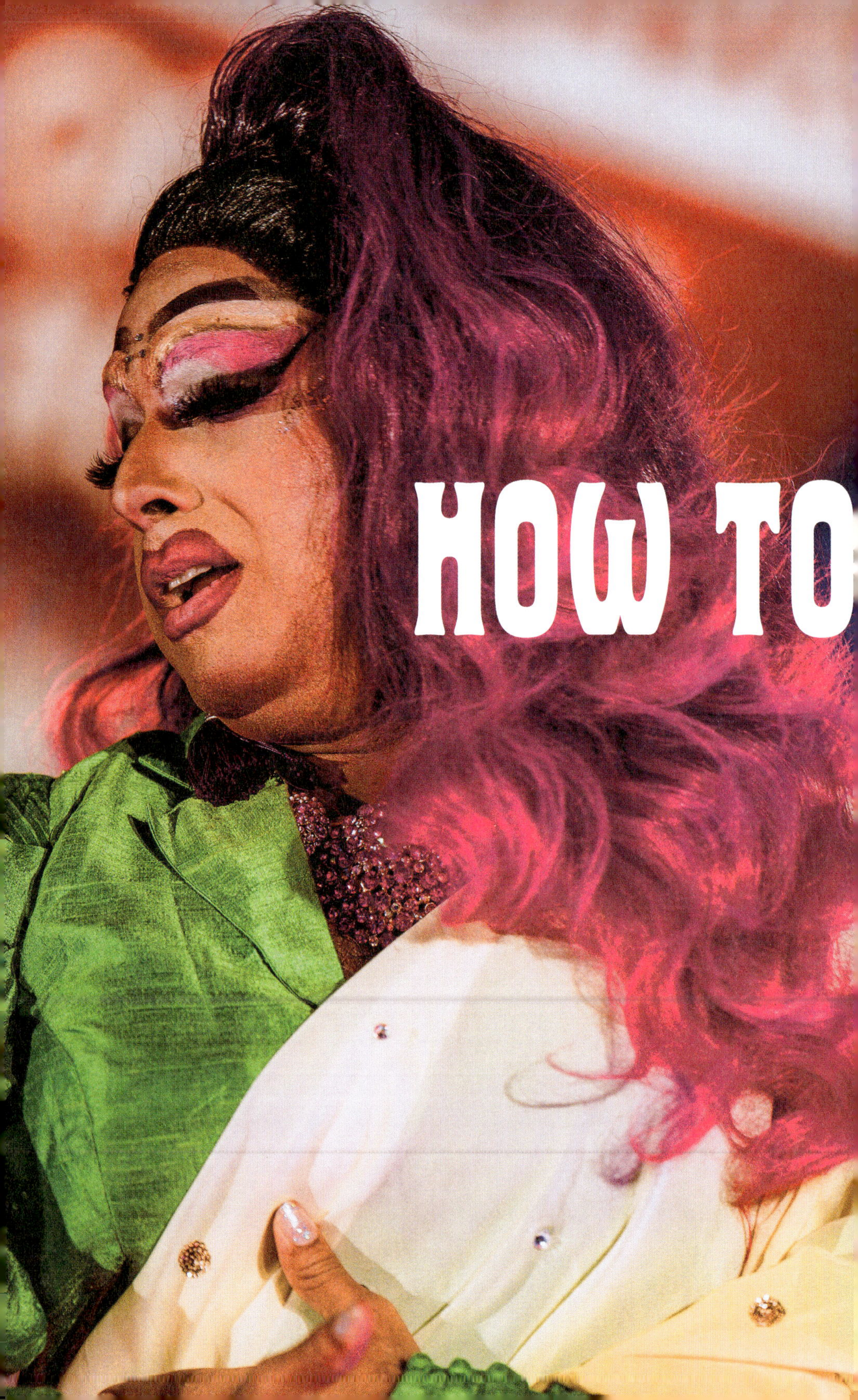

GRIEVE

Eight years later, and you're still doing that number!

Don't come for me doctor have the times changed?

No. They've only gotten worse.

Genocides and femicides on every continent.

Right-wing fascism everywhere.

Murders and disappearances of minoritized people go ignored and uninvestigated.

Bodily autonomies are curtailed.

Protest is suppressed.

Borders are even more militarized.

Carceral systems expand.

Healthcare services contract.

Corporations dictate our social,
political,and planetary futures.

How do we hold it together?

It's like there's nothing good
I just
LaWhore

Kareem 💔
that's why we have each other
to hold each other in joy and in grief
isn't that the point of drag?

Performing in the wake of the Muslim ban was not easy. But here I am writing at the dawn of Trump's second term, cringing at his promises to eviscerate so many forms of social, intellectual, and bodily autonomy. That "Damadam Mast Qalandar" performance may be eight years old, but it hasn't actually aged, has it? LaWhore created that number to make space for individual and communal grief. Queer and trans and immigrant and Indigenous and POC communities are flooded with grief. We are constantly losing rights, freedoms, and access to the basic things that make life livable. Our loved ones are taken from us by suicide, murder, epidemics, incarceration, deportation, and genocide. My friend and mentor Joshua Chambers-Letson reminds me, in his meditation on queer love and loss, that "the art of living with grief is about finding ways to live with loss as well as to work with it in the service of continuance and living on." He uses art to theorize grief, as well as to grieve. The art he witnesses and writes about makes room for him to encounter loss. For me, drag has been the art that helps me encounter loss, to work with it in service of living on.

Drag artists are no strangers to grief, and neither is our practice. According to Ocean Vuong, drag performers are uniquely positioned to interface with loss: "grief, at its worst, is unreal. And it calls for a surreal response. The queens—in this way—are unicorns. Unicorns stamping in a graveyard." Maybe this is why a ballad during a drag show is rarely disruptive. Kicks, splits, jumps, reveals, and gags can be followed by a dirge, and the audience will gently drop into the depressive stillness. It makes sense. As much as queer and trans people come to the club in search of pleasure and desire, we also sought this collectivity out of alienation, rejection, and heartbreak. We are ready for ritual. As much as queer and trans people come to the club in search of pleasure and desire, we also sought this collectivity out of alienation, rejection, and heartbreak.

As much as queer and trans people come to the club in search of pleasure and desire, we also sought this collectivity out of alienation, rejection, and heartbreak.

> *May 2015. Austin International Drag Festival.* The Iron Bear, Austin. Two members of the Black drag king troupe Momma's Boyz opened their set by remembering Black people who have been killed by police, pouring out a libation in memory of lost community members before singing the Civil Rights anthem "Oh Freedom!"

> *February 2024. Open to All.* 3 Dollar Bill, Brooklyn. At this weekly ball, staged at a nightclub where anyone interested in ball culture can come and witness the event, the emcee memorializes O'Shae Sibley. In 2023, Sibley was gay-bashed and murdered for voguing outside of a gas station in Brooklyn. *Open to All* (OTA) invoked Sibley's name to remind the community about the need for a sacred space in which gender-transgressive dance is safe and affirmed.

> *September 2023. Bushwig.* The Knockdown Center, Brooklyn. An altar is set up in honor of Simone Babes Trust, one of the founders of this massive drag festival who passed away that

summer. Also, at this show, Arab drag queen Rify Royalty performs Sinéad O'Connor's "Nothing Compares 2 U." This was a double tribute. To Sinéad, an artist who sacrificed her career speaking up for victims of sexual violence, Palestinians, people with mental health issues, and more—she had passed in July. But also a tribute to Rify's mother, who had passed the same month.

June 2017. *Drag Race*, Season 9 Finale. Los Angeles. In a lip-synch battle with Shea Couleé, Sasha Velour lifts the fire-red wig off her head during Whitney Houston's "I Get So Emotional." As Sasha shakes out the wig, a cascade of red rose petals falls around her, revealing her white, bald head. While Sasha has been bald throughout the competition, this reveal stages her hairless head as beautiful and powerful. This iconic and widely memed performance, and more generally her use of a bald head in her drag, is a tribute to the resilience of her late mother, who lost her hair during chemotherapy.

October 2023. Night Gallery, Los Angeles. Tommy Tonight, the drag king persona of artist Tomashi Jackson, performs throughout the gallery in front of Jackson's own visual artworks. Tommy lip-synchs across the Doobie Brothers' repertoire, her late mother's favorite. The soundtrack also interweaves an interview between Jackson and her mother recorded in 2010, and testimonials of a nurse losing patients during the height of the Covid pandemic. Tommy Tonight's lip-synch, soundscape, movement, and stillness draw attention to ongoing histories of racialized labor, intergenerational exchange, and multiple instances of isolation and loss.

August 2022. Cameo App. Kerri Colby sends me a video message. "Now Mister Kareem. I had to come up on here. I know I was supposed to record this yesterday when I was all glam

> and sparkly, because I know you like them glam and sparkles. But sometimes life has a way of testing you. Speaking of testing, honey, we are getting through it. We are both stepping through it in glory, and honor, and sparkle. I know it might be a little tough right now, but that's why it's time to keep going, keep moving, keep tipping them go-go dancers, and have fun. And you know what, watch you a couple of good movies. My favorite one is *Devil Wears Prada,* because 'Emilyyyyyy. Emilyyy. Emily.'"

My friends had arranged for *Drag Race* alum Kerri Colby to send me a little videogram to lift my spirits in the hardest of times. They knew drag was the only thing that would cut through my grief and reach me at my heart. My mother passed away in June 2022 after an almost two-year struggle with breast cancer. In 2007, she managed to beat it. But in this second bout, she was diagnosed at Stage 4, in October 2020, when pandemic lockdowns made access to travel and care difficult.

My mother was everything to me. Losing her was like losing a compass. I felt, I feel, directionless without her. Drag allows me to encounter grief through my body, to approach loss with honesty and materiality. It also lets me pursue beauty in the spirit with which Mum moved through the world.

Her name was Shoba Khubchandani, née Shobha Mahtani. She was born in Pune, India in 1949, and she grew up in Gibraltar. As a teenager, she traveled to Bombay with her parents during wedding season so that she could be matched with a boy. In 1970, she married my father and moved to Accra, Ghana. In 2002, my parents retired in Bangalore. Navigating many diasporas, she spoke English, Hindi, Sindhi, Spanish, and French. Over the course of her lifetime she was a housewife, restaurant manager, fine jewelry saleswoman, furniture importer, yoga teacher, spiritual advisor, and bespoke fashion designer. She was a very good mother, friend, and aunty.

Because I was the youngest of three boys, parenting me was easy for her. My brothers bore the brunt of her youthful anxiety around motherhood. Having done it twice already, she found me a breeze. She treated me with a soft hand. I was anyways very soft. In Ghana, where I grew up, she allowed me to accompany her to fabric and jewelry stores after picking me up from school. To tailors and gossip sessions with other aunties. To grocery stores where cashiers told us we looked like brother and sister.

My mother was radiant. She put a lot of effort into being beautiful—hair coloring treatments, cosmetic dentistry, various kinds of diets and fasts, yoga mornings. But her biggest investment was apparel: clothing, jewelry, shoes, bags. She had a stylist's eye for color and shape, and she kept up with global trends through *Cosmopolitan* and *Libas* magazines. The relationship and sex advice columns in these magazines, the agony aunts, counseled me through puberty. I spent many Friday evenings watching my mother get ready for fancy events, marveling as she brought out the pantheon of high-end saris and fine jewelry in order to decide what to wear.

My mother and I leaned on each other when my father fell into a suicidal depression. My brothers were away in college. My father spoke to no one, but watched TV in a drunken stupor, branding his arms with cigarette burns to test if he was still alive. When home felt particularly dangerous, we drove to the takeout restaurant Dolly's and bought Aunty Rani's famous spring rolls. They came in a long skinny bag. The bottom half of the bag contained taste-annihilating chili sauce. This section was tied off, and the spring roll sat on top. We would laugh in the car, trying to untie the bags and dip the spring roll as neatly as possible to avoid staining our clothes with the red-orange oil of the chili paste. Burning our palettes with freshly fried pastry and peppery sauce, huffing into the snack to cool it down, giggling at our failed attempts to keep our clothes stain-free was a perfect distraction from home. Eating spring rolls in the car, we made a different kind of home.

I kept secrets for my mother. If I was present when a jewelry client was paying her, she'd whisper, "Don't tell your father, OK?" The cash she hid away paid my college fees; my travels to India in the summer; her travels to visit family in Indonesia, Nairobi, Gibraltar, Spain, the UK; her vacations to Italy and Bangkok; her ever-expanding wardrobe. Money that my father didn't know about didn't need to be spent on the house or the car or computer upgrades or a ninth iPad.

When my mother realized that I could make use of her saris she started gifting them to me, glad to help style me as a classy socialite, not a tacky cabaret queen.

I kept secrets from my mother. Not about being queer. But I never spoke with her about my dating life, my crushes, my hookups, my sadness, my body image issues. My mother knew I did drag, but she didn't necessarily care for it. She didn't see my drag as wondrous or powerful. She wondered instead why I leaned toward tacky shiny fabrics ("Because they look good onstage, Mum!"). But she did take me shopping for said fabrics, making futile attempts to reign in my gaudy aesthetics. She took me to her tailor to make drag outfits, ensuring that zippers made quick changes easy, that there was space for my padded hips and bust.

And when she realized that I could make use of her saris she started gifting them to me. Unlike all the other glamorous garments she owned, these ones could fit me. She was glad to help style me as a classy socialite and not a tacky cabaret queen. Mum had a lot of saris. She rarely bought ready-made. Instead, she sourced chiffons, georgettes, and nets, then had them dyed, embroidered, and beaded to render the fashionable aesthetic she wanted. She only wore them for weddings or special occasions, and once a sari was worn and photographed it couldn't really be sported again. So, she'd sell them to friends and clients, repurpose them into other garments, or, if I caught her early enough during my annual Bangalore visits, give them to me.

When I wear mum's saris in drag I have a different awareness of my body. I have to take care of these $400 garments. The saris I wore when

I first started doing drag were ten-dollar polyester yardage, digitally printed or embellished with machine embroidery. My mother's saris are silk, hand-embroidered, and artisanally dyed. I know the labor that went into them. I often accompanied her to *karigars* (artisans), tailors, and dyers across Bangalore. Sometimes they came over to our house, and I served them chai while they sat with Mum at the dining table designing these outfits. Wearing Mum's saris to perform makes me aware not only of my own body, but of her, of her *work*. Not just the labor it took to make the beautiful things I'm wearing, but all the other work she had to do—the secrets she had to keep, the smiles she had to force, the risks she had to take—to afford the saris in the first place.

Mum loved to reorganize her cupboards. Her clothes were her prized items, the rings to her Gollum. When I visited her in the summer of 2021, after a major Covid wave in India had finally subsided, we sat in her dressing room to play with her Precious-es. We reorganized all her closets. We'd done that several times before. She loved organizing and rearranging cupboards and drawers. This time, though, the process was different. We weren't just *looking* at clothes; she was deciding what their future would be. It was an end-of-life practice. She put away the *nice* clothes that she wouldn't be able to wear because of Covid, because there was nowhere nice to go anymore. "These, make sure Farzana and Jenny get a first look at them before anyone else." She wasn't planning on wearing them ever again.

Her wedding saris came out from underneath piles of sweaters. They hadn't been worn in fifty years. Georgette saris with hand-applied gold sequins, pink-red for the ceremony and chocolate brown for the reception. "What am I supposed to do with these? You want them?" It wasn't

Wearing Mum's saris to perform makes me aware not only of my own body, but of her, of the work she did to feel beautiful.

a ceremonious "You were supposed to have these," or "I want to gift these to my daughters-in-law." Mum was a fashion girl, and she'd never force her daughters-in-law to wear an heirloom piece just because it had sentimental value to her. But I was there. Her little drag queen who could *actually* make use of these garments, who could keep them alive. She hated wasting things. These saris sat at the bottom of my closet for a while, and I would talk to any artist who would listen to me how I might frame them, preserve them on my walls somehow. But my friend Nikita, a textile artist and designer, suggested LaWhore wear them. "But they're her wedding saris?!" "So? Saris were meant to be worn." So now I wear them.

One of the saris that I pulled down from a difficult-to-reach shelf after she passed was a turquoise-blue satin sari, with a wide embroidered border of lilies in the same fabric. This sari was famously photographed at a 1980s *Diwali Ball* in Accra. Mum was the emcee. When I say "famously" I mean famous to our family. Turquoise was her favorite color. She felt good in that look, and mounted photos of herself wearing it in multiple frames in our childhood homes. The sari itself was party-stained and not particularly wearable. So, I had the border removed and attached to new fabric—I learned to repurpose clothes from *her*. Emceeing a drag brunch in her *Diwali Ball* sari, I felt iconic. I felt like those photos of her all around the house: smiling, and beautiful, the audience eating out of the palm of her hand.

LaWhore's audiences regularly "Awww" when I tell them that the garment I'm wearing was my mother's or was designed by her. She designed the leopard jumpsuit I use in the first act of *Lessons in Drag*, and even styled it with a belt and beaded necklace. My seafoam net sari that I wore on stage with Sasha Velour used to be hers—Mum had it pre-pleated and added Velcro so that I could use it for a quick change. And she took me shopping for the turquoise Anarkali that I use in the Muslim ban number. When audiences "Awww," I know they're reacting to the sweetness of a desi mother accepting and supporting her queer child to the extent she was willing to style him as a gorgeous drag queen. But that wasn't exactly our relationship. She wasn't an "ally." It's not a word she knew, nor one I taught her. She rarely talked with me or others about queerness. She was always surprised to learn that any new friend or colleague in my life was queer. My drag remained a mystery to her, even after she saw LaWhore perform in Bangalore: "Is that really you under there? Under the makeup? I don't recognize you!"

Drag gives me a reason, a conceit, an occasion to use her saris, gives me more opportunities to be with her after she is gone.

For me, Drag gives me a reason, a conceit, an occasion to use her saris, gives me more opportunities to be with her after she is gone. I receive the audience's generosity, their "Awww," not as an acknowledgment of her emotional labor, but rather as their recognition of my reverence for her. I let the audience's warm feeling take me back to her everyday labor of living beautifully. She loved beautiful things; she wanted a hand in making them so. She worked very hard in order to access beauty.

When I wear my mother's saris in drag, I don't attempt to look *like* her. I camp up the look with over-styled blonde hair, a heavily embellished blouse, or knife-sharp nails. I performed with her garments even before she passed. But when I wear them, I get to remember how she lived. Using her saris now gives me more opportunities to be with her after she is gone. Drag gives me a reason, a conceit, an occasion to wear these heavily embellished garments. They give me something to touch and feel. They continue to make me in the ways that she did.

Since Mum passed, I've added a small edit to the *Lessons in Drag* show. After the Muslim ban number, I show a clip from that New Jersey wedding in which my aunties sing "Damadam Mast Qalandar" to the groom's mother. It works nicely there to bridge the section on "Aunties" with that on "Race and Religion" and create continuity in the show. But, more importantly, for ninety seconds I get to watch my mother on screen, singing and clapping and preventing the mother of the groom from knocking over a glass of red wine. It's one of few soft moments for me in the show in which I'm not speaking, quick-changing, or doing a number. I just get to be with her as she claps, and smiles, and sings with a chorus of aunties who have known and loved each other for decades:

Ho laal meri pat,
Rakhiyon bala jhoole laalan
Sindhri da, Sehwan da
Sakhi shabaaz qalandar
Damadam mast qalandar
Ali da pehla number
Sakhi shabaaz qalandar
Ho laj meri, ho laj meri.

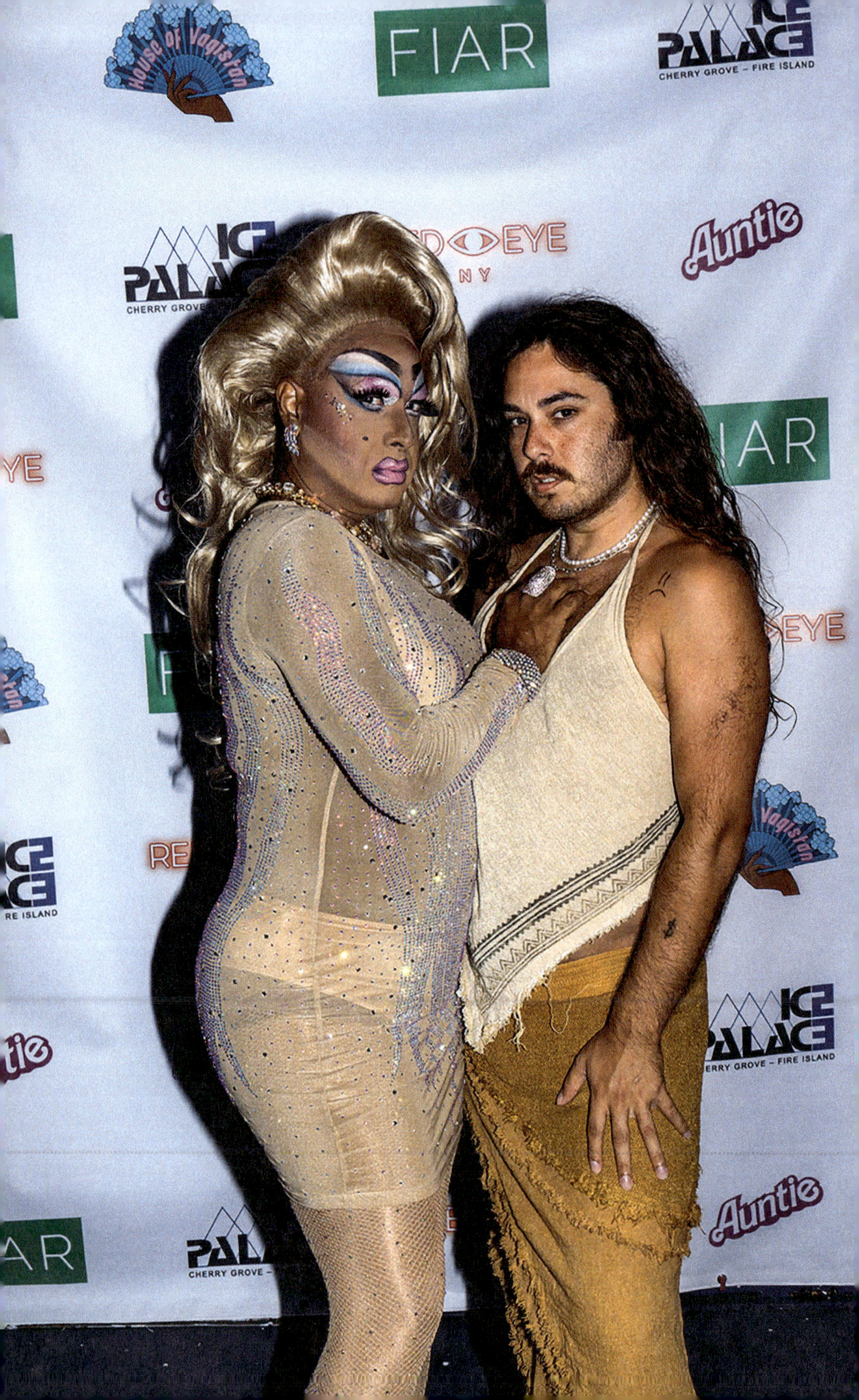

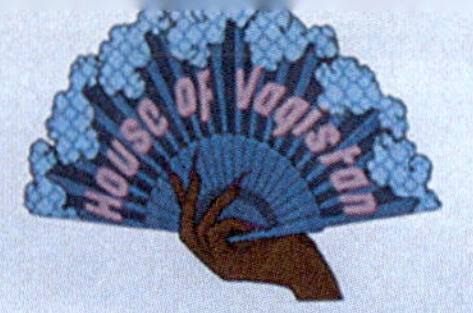
House of Vagistan

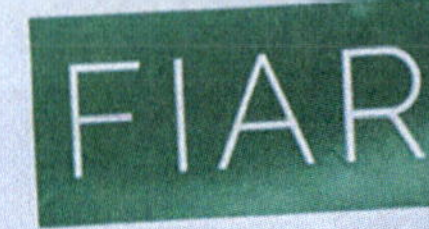
FIAR

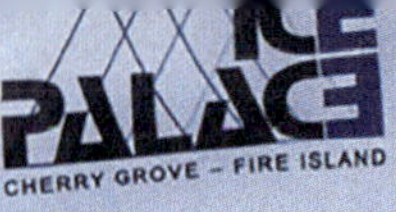
ICE
PALACE
CHERRY GROVE – FIRE ISLAND

ACKNOWLEDGMENTS

This project was born out of an invitation from Ulka Anjaria to speak and perform at Brandeis University in 2022 as part of the Mandel Lectures in the Humanities series. Thank you, Ulka, and all your colleagues at the Mandel Center, for taking a risk with this invitation. This book benefited immensely from the generous editorial work at Brandeis University Press: Sue Ramin, Ashley Burns, Natalie Jones, Ann Brash, Jim Schley, Mindy Basinger Hill, Maxine Rosenfeld, and the most gracious Reviewer No. 1, whose feedback encouraged both clarity and creativity, a rare gift from the often depersonalized peer review process. Though written in a short span of time, this book looks and feels robust because of brilliant developmental editing by Joshua Williams (williamseditorial.com)—don't hesitate, hire him!

The show *Lessons in Drag* that forms the foundation of this book has evolved and grown over the last ten years thanks to the generosity of colleagues who have taken the effort to invite the show to their institutions, raise funds, book spaces, launch publicity, and arrange logistics. Thank you for all that administrative labor, and for taking the risk to make room for drag in the academy and beyond.

I hope, readers, that you've spent time marveling at the gorgeous photographs in this book! Follow these brilliant and talented photographers—Mettie Ostrowski, Tim Correira, Justin Barbin, nik lee, RuAfza, Steve Osemwenkhae, Koitz, Davide Laffe—on social media and book them for your shoots.

The ideas and shape of this book come from encounters with many scholarly and creative interlocutors: Brian Horton, Rhonda Jewels, Sabel Scities, Ryan Persadie, Jacob Bird, Uzma Zafar, Enzo Toral, Gautham Reddy, Kamani Sutra, Nikita Untitle, Vyjayanthi Vadrevu, RuAfza, Aster R*sk, Kulfi Jaan, Chai Treason, Emi Grate, Candace Persuasion, Sasha Velour, Johnny Velour, Kerri Colby, Raja, Alok, Ali Sethi, Malai, Mac Irvine, Teri Incampo, Jenny Henderson, Gowri

Vijayakumar, Dwai Banerjee, Summer Kim Lee, Kemi Adeyemi, Lily Mengesha, Chris Lloyd, AB Brown, Nikki Yeboah, Hope Freeman, Durba Mitra, Akhil Kang, Poorna Swami, Zirwat Chowdhury, Jeff Roy, Pavithra Prasad, Christine Mok, Clare Croft, Al Evangelista, Naisargi Dave, Johnny Estrella, Robert Ramirez, Jesus I. Valles, Nidhi Mahajan, Lindsey Blair Cooke, Joe Parslow, Marwan Kaabour, the Boy Luck Club, the Pink Divas, Fire Island Artist Residency, Trikone-Chicago, the *Jai Ho!* team, the cast of *Dragistan*, the House of Vagistan, the New England Theatre and Performance Studies seminar at Harvard's Mahindra Center, and the Tufts Faculty Research Awards Committee.

I offer this book in memory of Deepa Patel, Ifti Nasim, Allison Powell, Tejas Pande, Danielle Abrams, and Jonathan Magat, friends who believed in the magic of drag, performance, and nightlife as much as I do. I hope you hear my fans clacking for you in the beautiful beyond!

WORKS CITED AND FURTHER READING

INTRODUCTION Lessons in Drag

Asif, Manan Ahmed. *Disrupted City: Walking the Pathways of Memory and History in Lahore*. New York: The New Press, 2024.

Berlant, Lauren, and Michael Warner. "What Does Queer Theory Teach Us About X?" *PMLA: Publications of the Modern Language Association of America* 110, no. 3 (1995): 343–49.

Bird, Jacob Mallinson. "Haptic Aurality: On Touching the Voice in Drag Lip-Sync Performance." *Sound Studies (2015)* 6, no. 1 (2020): 45–64.

Butler, Judith. *Gender Trouble: Feminism and the Subversion of Identity*. New York: Routledge, 1990.

Dhalla, Ghalib Shiraz. *Ode to Lata*. Los Angeles: Really Great Books, 2002.

Dolan, Jill. *Utopia in Performance: Finding Hope at the Theater*. Ann Arbor: University of Michigan Press, 2008.

Dolmage, Jay. *Academic Ableism: Disability and Higher Education*. Ann Arbor: University of Michigan Press, 2018.

Dutta, Nandita. "Drag Queen in the Beauty Salon: What Theorising Strange Bedfellows Can Tell Us About the Labour of Aunties." *South Asia* 46, no. 1 (2023): 218–33.

Edward, Mark. "Drag Kings and Queens of Higher Education." In *Contemporary Drag Practices and Performers: Drag in a Changing Scene, Volume 1*, edited by Mark Edward and Stephen Farrier. London, Bloomsbury Publishing, 2020.

Falzon, Mark-Anthony. *Cosmopolitan Connections: The Sindhi Diaspora, 1860–2000*. Leiden: Brill, 2004.

Ferguson, Roderick A. *The Reorder of Things: The University and Its Pedagogies of Minority Difference*. Minneapolis: University of Minnesota Press, 2012.

García-Peña Lorgia. *Community as Rebellion: A Syllabus for Surviving Academia as a Woman of Color*. Chicago: Haymarket Books, 2022.

Gilroy, Paul. *The Black Atlantic: Modernity and Double Consciousness*. Cambridge, MA: Harvard University Press, 1993.

Goodman, Elyssa Maxx. *Glitter and Concrete: A Cultural History of Drag in New York City*. Toronto: Hanover Square Press, 2023.

Gopinath, Gayatri. *Impossible Desires: Queer Diasporas and South Asian Public Cultures*. Durham: Duke University Press, 2005.

Heller, Meredith. *Queering Drag: Redefining the Discourse of Gender-Bending*. Bloomington: Indiana University Press, 2020.

Hutcheon, Linda. *A Theory of Adaptation*. New York: Routledge, 2006.

Jackson, Shannon. *Professing Performance: Theatre in the Academy from Philology to Performativity*. New York: Cambridge University Press, 2004.

Johnson, E. Patrick. *Appropriating Blackness: Performance and the Politics of Authenticity*. Durham: Duke University Press, 2003.

Johnson, E. Patrick. *Sweet Tea: Black Gay Men of the South*. Chapel Hill: University of North Carolina Press, 2008.

Kalivis, George. "Becoming a Manual: Au(n)to-Ethnography and Queer Performances of a Greek Theía." *Text and Performance Quarterly* 42, no. 3 (2022): 298–314.

Khubchandani, Kareem. *Decolonize Drag*. New York: OR Books, 2023.

Khubchandani, Kareem. *Ishtyle: Accenting Gay Indian Nightlife*. Ann Arbor: University of Michigan Press, 2020.

Khubchandani, Kareem. "Lessons in Drag: An Interview with Lawhore Vagistan." *Theatre Topics* 25, no. 3 (2015): 285–94.

Kureishi, Hanif. *The Buddha of Suburbia*. New York: Viking, 1990.

Lim, Eng-Beng. "Performing the Global University." *Social Text* 27, no. 4 (2009): 25–44.

Luna, Caleb. "The Gender Nonconformity of My Fatness." 2018, accessed October 31, 2020, https://thebodyisnotanapology.com/magazine/the-gender-nonconformity-of-my-fatness/.

Madison, D. Soyini. "It's Time to Write: Writing as Performance." In *Critical Ethnography: Method, Ethics, and Performance*. Thousand Oaks, CA: Sage Publications (2005): 181–99.

Madison, D. Soyini. "Performing Ethnography: The Political Economy of Water." *Performance Research* 12, no. 3, (2007): 16–27.

Markovits, Claude. *The Global World of Indian Merchants, 1750–1947: Traders of Sind from Bukhara to Panama*. New York: Cambridge University Press, 2000.

McGlotten, Shaka. *Dragging: Or, in the Drag of a Queer Life*. New York: Routledge, 2019.

McMillan, Uri. *Embodied Avatars: Genealogies of Black Feminist Art and Performance*. New York: New York University Press, 2015.

Mitchell, Nick. "(Critical Ethnic Studies) Intellectual." *Critical Ethnic Studies* 1, no. 1 (2015): 86–94.

Muñoz, José Esteban. *Disidentifications: Queers of Color and the Performance of Politics*. Minneapolis: University of Minnesota Press, 1999.

Newton, Esther. *Mother Camp: Female Impersonators in America*. Chicago: University of Chicago Press, 1979.

Peterson, Eric E., and Kristin M. Langellier. "The Politics of Personal Narrative Methodology." *Text and Performance Quarterly* 17, no. 2 (1997): 135–52.

Puar, Jasbir K. *Terrorist Assemblages: Homonationalism in Queer Times*. Durham: Duke University Press, 2007.

Ramey, Steven Wesley. *Hindu, Sufi, or Sikh: Contested Practices and Identifications of Sindhi Hindus in India and Beyond*. New York: Palgrave Macmillan, 2008.

Rogers, Baker A. *King of Hearts: Drag Kings in the American South*. New Brunswick: Rutgers University Press, 2021.

Rupp, Leila J and Verta Taylor. *Drag Queens at the 801 Cabaret*. Chicago: University of Chicago Press, 2015.

Satyal, Rakesh. *Blue Boy*. New York: Kensington Books, 2009.

Schwartz, Selby Wynn. *The Bodies of Others: Drag Dances and Their Afterlives*. Ann Arbor: University of Michigan Press, 2019.

Scott, Joan. "The Evidence of Experience." *Critical Inquiry* 17, no. 4 (1991): 773–797.

Spruill, Jennifer. "Ad/Dressing the Nation: Drag and Authenticity

in Post-Apartheid South Africa." *Journal of Homosexuality* 46, no. 3–4 (2004): 91–111.
Strings, Sabrina. *Fearing the Black Body: The Racial Origins of Fat Phobia*. New York: New York University Press, 2019.
Wilson, Ara. *The Intimate Economies of Bangkok: Tomboys, Tycoons, and Avon Ladies in the Global City*. Berkeley: University of California Press, 2004.

CHAPTER ONE How to Do Research

Arondekar, Anjali R. *Abundance: Sexuality's History*. Durham: Duke University Press, 2023.
Berlant, Lauren Gail. *The Queen of America Goes to Washington City: Essays on Sex and Citizenship*. Durham: Duke University Press, 1997.
Connerton, Paul. *How Societies Remember*. New York: Cambridge University Press, 1989.
Conquergood, Dwight, and E. Patrick Johnson. *Cultural Struggles: Performance, Ethnography, Praxis*. Ann Arbor: University of Michigan Press, 2013.
Draper, Jimmy. "'What Has She Actually Done??!': Gay Men, Diva Worship, and the Paratextualization of Gay–Rights Support." *Critical Studies in Media Communication* 34, no. 2 (2017): 130–37.
Fairfield, Joy Brooke, and Enzo Vasquez Toral. "Cuir Devotion: A Conversation." *Ecumenica* 13, no. 1 (2020): 81–100.
Feminist Critical Hindu Studies Collective. "Auntylectuals: A Nonce Taxonomy of Aunty-Power." *Text and Performance Quarterly* 42, no. 3 (2022): 346–57.
Franklin, Adrian. "Performing Live." *Tourist Studies* 1, no. 3 (2001): 211–32.
Iyer, Usha. *Dancing Women: Choreographing Corporeal Histories of Hindi Cinema*. New York: Oxford University Press, 2020.
Jaime, Karen. "'Dance with Me in the Disco Heat': Nowhere Bar's Temporal Shifts." In *Queer Nightlife*, edited by Kemi Adeyemi, Ka-

reem Khubchandani and Ramón H. Rivera–Servera, 76–82. Ann Arbor: University of Michigan Press, 2021.

Johnson, E. Patrick. "From Page to Stage: The Making of Sweet Tea." *Text and Performance Quarterly* 32, no. 3 (2012): 248–53.

Khubchandani, Kareem. "Aunty Fever: A Queer Impression." In *Queer Dance: Meanings and Makings*, edited by Clare Croft, 199–204. New York: Oxford University Press, 2017.

Khubchandani, Kareem. "Between Aunties: Sexual Futures and Queer South Asian Aunty Porn." *Porn Studies* (2021): 1–19.

Khubchandani, Kareem. "Bollywood Affects: Feeling Brown with Meena Kumari." In *Theatre After Empire*, edited by Harvey Young and Megan Geigner, 177–92. London: Routledge, 2021.

Khubchandani, Kareem. "Critical Aunty Studies: An Auntroduction." *Text and Performance Quarterly* 42, no. 3 (2022): 221–45.

Khubchandani, Kareem. "Dance Floor Divas: Fieldwork, Fabulating and Fathoming in Queer Bangalore." *South Asia: Journal of South Asian Studies* (2020): 1–12.

Kim Lee, Summer. "Borrowed Speech: Giving an Account of Another with Wu Tsang's Full Body Quotation." *ASAP Journal* 6, no. 3 (2021): 679–706.

Koestenbaum, Wayne. *The Queen's Throat: Opera, Homosexuality, and the Mystery of Desire*. New York: Poseidon Press, 1993.

Luvaas, Brent. "Unbecoming: The Aftereffects of Autoethnography." *Ethnography* 20, no. 2 (2019): 245–62.

Musser, Amber Jamilla. "Between Shine and Porosity." *Social Text* 41, no. 2 (2023): 1–18.

Muñoz, José Esteban. "Stages: Queers, Punks, and the Utopian Performative." In *The Sage Handbook of Performance Studies*, edited by D. Soyini Madison and Judith Hamera, 9–20. Thousand Oaks, CA: Sage, 2006.

Narayan, Kirin, Smadar Lavie, and Renato Rosaldo. *Creativity/Anthropology*. Ithaca, NY: Cornell University Press, 2018.

Newton, Esther. "My Best Informant's Dress: The Erotic Equation in Fieldwork." *Cultural Anthropology* 8, no. 1 (1993): 3–23.

Paredez, Deborah. *Selenidad: Selena, Latinos, and the Performance of Memory*. Durham: Duke University Press, 2009.

Parslow, Joe. *Their Majesty: Drag Performance and Queer Communities in London*. Abingdon: Routledge, 2024.

Persadie, Ryan. "Queering 'Queer' Toronto Space: Transgressive QT-BIPOC Drag Artists and Disrupting Homonormativity." *Canadian Theatre Review* 185 (2021): 22–28.

Ryan, Persadie. "Tanty Feminisms: The Aesthetics of Auntyhood, #Coolieween and the Erotics of Post-Indenture." *Journal of Indentureship and Its Legacies* 2, no. 1 (2022): 59–97.

Sangarasivam, Yamuna. "Researcher, Informant, 'Assassin,' Me." *Geographical Review* 91, no. 1–2 (2001): 95–104.

Stonely, Peter. *A Queer History of the Ballet*. New York: Routledge, 2007.

Thompson, Krista A. *Shine: The Visual Economy of Light in African Diasporic Aesthetic Practice*. Durham: Duke University Press, 2015.

Tincknell, Estella. "Monstrous Aunties: The Rabelaisian Older Asian Woman in British Cinema and Television Comedy." *Feminist Media Studies* 20, no. 1 (2020): 135–50.

Visweswaran, Kamala. *Fictions of Feminist Ethnography*. Minneapolis: University of Minnesota Press, 1994.

Weiss, Margot. "The Interlocutor Slot: Citing, Crediting, Cotheorizing, and the Problem of Ethnographic Expertise." *American Anthropologist* 123, no. 4 (2021): 948–53.

Wolf, Stacy. "'Defying Gravity': Queer Conventions in the Musical 'Wicked.'" *Theatre Journal* 60, no. 1 (2008): 1–21.

CHAPTER TWO How to Be a Drag Queen

Al-Kadhi, Amrou. *Unicorn: The Memoir of a Muslim Drag Queen*. London: Fourth Estate, 2019.

Banerjee, Mukulika, and Daniel Miller. *The Sari*. Oxford: Berg, 2003.

Blair, Zachary. "Boystown: Gay Neighborhoods, Social Media, and the (Re)Production of Racism." In *No Tea No Shade: New Writings in Black Queer Studies*, edited by E. Patrick Johnson, 287–303. Durham: Duke University Press, 2020.

Brennan, Niall, and David Gudelunas. *RuPaul's Drag Race and the Shifting Visibility of Drag Culture: The Boundaries of Reality TV*. Cham: Springer International Publishing AG, 2017.

Campana, Mario, Katherine Duffy, Mikko Laamanen, Maria Rita Micheli, and Rohan Venkatraman. *Drag as Marketplace: Contemporary Cultures, Identities, and Business*. Bristol: Bristol University Press, 2024.

Dasgupta, Rohit, Churnjeet Mahn, and DJ Ritu. *Desi Queers: LGBTQ+ South Asians and Cultural Belonging in Britain*. London: Hurst & Company, 2025.

Dolan, Jill. *Utopia in Performance: Finding Hope at the Theater*. Ann Arbor: University of Michigan Press, 2008.

Goodman, Elyssa Maxx. *Glitter and Concrete: A Cultural History of Drag in New York City*. Toronto: Hanover Square Press, 2023.

Heller, Meredith. *Queering Drag: Redefining the Discourse of Gender-Bending*. Bloomington: Indiana University Press, 2020.

La Fountain-Stokes, Lawrence. *Translocas: The Politics of Puerto Rican Drag and Trans Performance*. Ann Arbor: University of Michigan Press, 2021.

McGlotten, Shaka. *Dragging: Or, in the Drag of a Queer Life*. New York: Routledge, 2019.

Menon, Jisha. *The Performance of Nationalism: India, Pakistan, and the Memory of Partition*. Cambridge: Cambridge University Press, 2013.

Paredez, Deborah. *Selenidad: Selena, Latinos, and the Performance of Memory*. Durham: Duke University Press, 2009.

Parslow, Joe. *Their Majesty: Drag Performance and Queer Communities in London*. Abingdon: Routledge, 2024.

Ramaswamy, Sumathi. *The Goddess and the Nation: Mapping Mother India*. Durham: Duke University Press, 2010.

Reddy, Gayatri. "Queer *Desi* Formations: Marking the Boundaries of Cultural Belonging in Chicago." In *Pakistan Desires: Queer Futures Elsewhere,* edited by Omar Kasmani, 216–35. Durham: Duke University Press, 2023.

Sinha, Mrinalini. *Specters of Mother India: The Global Restructuring of an Empire*. Durham: Duke University Press, 2006.

Tagle, Thea Quiray. "'I Will Always Love You': Queer Filipino Performance of Blackness, Death, and Return." In *Q & A: Voices from Queer Asian North America,* edited by Martin Manalansan, Alice Y. Hom, Kale B. Fajardo, and David L. Eng, 343–51. Philadelphia: Temple University Press, 2021.

Velour, Sasha. *The Big Reveal: An Illustrated Manifesto of Drag*. New York: Harper, 2023.

CHAPTER THREE How to Teach

Academic Aunties, www.academicaunties.com.

Ahmed, Sara. *On Being Included: Racism and Diversity in Institutional Life*. Durham: Duke University Press, 2012.

Chuh, Kandice. "On (Not) Mentoring." Social Text online, 2013, accessed 2024, https://socialtextjournal.org/periscope_article/on-not-mentoring/.

Cox, Aimee Meredith. *Shapeshifters: Black Girls and the Choreography of Citizenship*. Durham: Duke University Press, 2015.

Dolan, Jill. *Geographies of Learning: Theory and Practice, Activism and Performance*. Middletown, CT: Wesleyan University Press, 2001.

Gallop, Jane. *Pedagogy: The Question of Impersonation*. Bloomington: Indiana University Press, 1995.

Gamboa, Eddie. "Pedagogies of the Dark: Making Sense of Queer Nightlife." In *Queer Nightlife,* edited by Kemi Adeyemi, Kareem Khubchandani, and Ramón H. Rivera-Servera, 76–82. Ann Arbor: University of Michigan Press, 2021.

Hale, C. Jacob. "Leatherdyke Boys and Their Daddies: How to Have

Sex without Women or Men." *Social Text*, no. 52/53 (1997): 223–36.

Hamera, Judith. "Exposing the Pedagogical Body: Protocols and Tactics." In *Performance Theories in Education: Power Pedagogy and the Politics of Identity*, edited by Bryant Keith Alexander, Gary L. Anderson, and Bernardo P. Gallegos, 63–81. London: Lawrence Erlbaum Associates, 2005.

Hankins, Sarah. "'I'm a Cross between a Clown, a Stripper, and a Streetwalker': Drag Tipping, Sex Work, and a Queer Sociosexual Economy." *Signs: Journal of Women in Culture and Society* 40, no. 2 (2015): 441–66.

Johnson, E. Patrick. "In the Merry Old Land of Oz: Race(e)ing and Quee(r)ing the Academy." In *The Queer Community: Continuing the Struggle for Social Justice*, edited by Richard Johnson, 85–104. San Diego: Birkdale Publishers, 2009.

Johnson, E. Patrick. "Performance and/as Pedagogy: Performing Blackness in the Classroom." In *Appropriating Blackness* by E. Patrick Johnson. 219–56. Durham: Duke University Press, 2020.

Keenan, Harper, and Lil Miss Hot Mess. "Drag Pedagogy: The Playful Practice of Queer Imagination in Early Childhood." *Curriculum Inquiry* 50, no. 5 (2020): 440–61.

Lewis, Mel Michelle. "A Genuine Article: Intersectionality, Black Lesbian Gender Expression, and the Feminist Pedagogical Project." *Journal of Lesbian Studies* 21, no. 4 (2017): 420–31.

MacNell, Lillian, Adam Driscoll, and Andrea N. Hunt. "What's in a Name: Exposing Gender Bias in Student Ratings of Teaching." *Innovative Higher Education* 40, no. 4 (2015): 291–303.

McGlotten, Shaka. *Dragging: Or, in the Drag of a Queer Life*. New York: Routledge, 2019.

Misra, Joya, Alexandra Kuvaeva, Kerryann O'meara, Dawn Kiyoe Culpepper, and Audrey Jaeger. "Gendered and Racialized Perceptions of Faculty Workloads." *Gender & Society* 35, no. 3 (2021): 358–94.

Montez, Noe, and Kareem Khubchandani. "A Note from the Editors: Queer Pedagogy in Theatre and Performance." *Theatre Topics* 30, no. 2 (2020): ix–xvii.

Musser, Amber. "Specimen Days: Diversity, Labor, and the University." *Feminist Formations* 27, no. 3 (2015): 1–20.

Newton, Esther. *Mother Camp: Female Impersonators in America.* Chicago: University of Chicago Press, 1979.

Patton, Cindy. *Fatal Advice: How Safe-Sex Education Went Wrong.* Durham: Duke University Press, 1996.

Senelick, Laurence. *The Changing Room: Sex, Drag, and Theatre.* New York: Routledge, 2000.

Shange, Savannah. "Play Aunties and Dyke Bitches: Gender, Generation, and the Ethics of Black Queer Kinship." *The Black Scholar* 49, no. 1 (2019): 40–54.

Stryker, Susan. "Dungeon Intimacies: The Poetics of Transsexual Sadomasochism." *Parallax* 14, no. 1 (2008): 36–47.

Testa, Nino. "How Do You Solve a Problem Like Maria von Clapp? Drag Pedagogy and the Limits of DEI." *WSQ: Women's Studies Quarterly* 53, no. 1 (2025): 91–113.

CHAPTER FOUR How to Be an Aunty

Alvarado, Lorena. "Never Late: Unwelcome Desires and Diasporas in Chavela Vargas' Last Works." *Women & Performance: A Journal of Feminist Theory* 26, no. 1 (2016): 17–35.

Akinbola, Bimbola. "Africanaunties: Performing Diasporic Digital Disbelongings on Tiktok." *Text and Performance Quarterly* 42, no. 3 (2022): 284–97.

Bailey, Marlon M. *Butch Queens up in Pumps: Gender, Performance, and Ballroom Culture in Detroit.* Ann Arbor: University of Michigan Press, 2013.

Ballakrishnen, Swethaa S. "Anti/Aunty as Critical Method: From Gendered Resistance to Soft Grace." *South Asia* 46, no. 1 (2023): 135–51.

Bhardwaj, Maya. "Bad Brown Aunties, Fagony Aunts and Resistance Aunties: Centring Queer Desi Aunties in Diasporic Social Movement and Justice Work." *South Asia* 46, no. 1 (2023): 113–34.

Brown, AB. "Tau(n)tology: Tannie Evita's Stewardship of South Africa's National Transitions." *Text and Performance Quarterly* 42, no. 3 (2022): 264–83.

Cobham-Sander, Rhonda. "Amital Queer: Aunts, Negresses, and Auntie Men in Dionne Brand's 'Dialectics' and Hilton Als's *The Women*." *Text and Performance Quarterly* 42, no. 3 (2022): 246–63.

Freeman, Elizabeth. *Time Binds: Queer Temporalities, Queer Histories*. Durham: Duke University Press, 2010.

Jha, Priya. "Remembering Nargis, Retelling Mother India: Criticism, Melodrama, and National Mythmaking." *South Asian Popular Culture* 9, no. 3 (2011): 287–97.

Johnson, E. Patrick. "Mother Knows Best: Blackness and Transgressive Domestic Space." In *Appropriating Blackness: Performance and the Politics of Authenticity*, 76–103. Durham: Duke University Press, 2003.

Khubchandani, Kareem. "Aunty Fever: A Queer Impression." In *Queer Dance: Meanings and Makings*, edited by Clare Croft, 199–204. New York: Oxford University Press, 2017.

Khubchandani, Kareem. "Between Aunties: Sexual Futures and Queer South Asian Aunty Porn." *Porn Studies* (2021): 1–19.

Khubchandani, Kareem. "Critical Aunty Studies: An Auntroduction." *Text and Performance Quarterly* 42, no. 3 (2022): 221–45.

Khubchandani, Kareem. "Bollywood Affects: Feeling Brown with Meena Kumari." In *Theatre After Empire*, edited by Megan Geigner and Harvey Young, 177–92. London: Routledge, 2021.

Lin, Minhui, Jigang Bao, and Erwei Dong. "Dancing in Public Spaces: An Exploratory Study on China's Grooving Grannies." *Leisure Studies* 39, no. 4 (2020): 545–57.

Loomba, Ania. "The Long and Saggy Sari." *Women* 8, no. 3 (1997): 278–92.

Manalansan, Martin. "Aunty in an Epidemic: A Conversation with Tita Aida." Critical Aunty Studies, 2020, accessed April 28, 2022, www.criticalauntystudies.com/08–drag.

Natalie, Sarrazin. "The Vocal Narratives of Lata Mangeshkar: Gender, Politics, and Nation in India." In *Social Voices: The Cultural Politics of Singers around the Globe*, edited by Levi S. Gibbs, 201-218. Champaign: University of Illinois Press, 2023.

Persadie, Ryan. "Tanty Feminisms: The Aesthetics of Auntyhood, #Coolieween and the Erotics of Post-Indenture." *Journal of Indentureship and Its Legacies* 2, no. 1 (2022): 59–97.

Pinto, Jerry. *Helen: The Life and Times of an H-Bomb*. New Delhi: Penguin Books, 2006.

Rivera-Servera, Ramón H. "History in Drag: Latina/o Queer Affective Circuits in Chicago." In *Latina/o Midwest Reader*, edited by Omar Valerio-Jiménez, Santiago R. Vaquera-Vásquez, and Claire F. Fox, 185–96. Champaign: University of Illinois Press, 2017.

Sandhu, Arti. "India's Digital Drag Aunties: Breaking New Ground Wearing Familiar Fashions." *Dress: Special Issue: LGBTQ+ Fashions, Styles, and Bodies* 45, no. 1 (2019): 55–73.

Sehlikoglu, Sertaç. *Working out Desire: Women, Sport, and Self-Making in Istanbul.* Syracuse: Syracuse University Press, 2021.

Solnit, Rebecca, and Kristina Wong. "A Short (but Meandering) History of the Auntie Sewing Squad by A.S.S. Founder and Overlord Kristina Wong in Conversation with Auntie Rebecca Solnit." Critical Aunty Studies, 2020, accessed April 28, 2022, www.criticalauntystudies.com/04–work.

CHAPTER FIVE How to Write

Alford, Robert R. *The Craft of Inquiry: Theories, Methods, Evidence.* New York: Oxford University Press, 1998.

Anderson, Patrick. *Autobiography of a Disease*. New York: Routledge, 2017.

Anjaria, Jonathan Shapiro, and Ulka Anjaria. "Mazaa: Rethinking Fun, Pleasure and Play in South Asia." *South Asia* 43, no. 2 (2020): 232–42.

Booth, Wayne C., and Gregory G. Colomb. *The Craft of Research*. Chicago: University of Chicago Press, 2003.

Chee, Alexander. *How to Write An Autobiographical Novel: Essays*. Boston: Houghton Mifflin Harcourt, 2018.

Christian, Barbara. "The Race for Theory." *Feminist Studies* 14, no. 1 (1988): 67–79.

Dutta, Nandita. "Drag Queen in the Beauty Salon: What Theorising Strange Bedfellows Can Tell Us About the Labour of Aunties." *South Asia* 46, no. 1 (2023): 218–33.

hooks, bell. *Teaching to Transgress: Education as the Practice of Freedom*. New York: Routledge, 1994.

Johnson, E. Patrick. *Honeypot: Black Southern Women Who Love Women*. Durham: Duke University Press, 2019.

McMillan, Uri. "Nicki-Aesthetics: The Camp Performance of Nicki Minaj." *Women & Performance* 24, no. 1 (2014): 79–87.

Muñoz, José Esteban. "Ephemera as Evidence: Introductory Notes to Queer Acts." *Women & Performance* 8, no. 2 (1996): 5–16.

Newton, Esther. *My Butch Career: A Memoir*. Durham: Duke University Press, 2018.

Phelan, Peggy. "A Second Take: On Performative Writing and Reading." *TDR: The Drama Review* 68, no. 2 (2024): 11–23.

Pollock, Della. "Performing Writing." In *The Ends of Performance*, edited by Peggy Phelan and Jill Lane, 73–103. New York: NYU Press, 1998.

Schechner, Richard. *Performance Studies: An Introduction*. New York: Routledge, 2006.

Sedgwick, Eve Kosofsky. *Touching Feeling: Affect, Pedagogy, Performativity*. Durham: Duke University Press, 2003.

Tinsley, Omise'eke Natasha. *Ezili's Mirrors: Imagining Black Queer Genders*. Durham: Duke University Press, 2018.

CHAPTER SIX How to Be a Map

Adeyemi, Kemi. "Donald Trump Is the Perfect Man for the Job." *QED* 4, no. 2 (2017): 56–62.

Anzaldúa, Gloria. *Borderlands / La Frontera*. 2nd ed. San Francisco: Aunt Lute Books, 1999.

Arondekar, Anjali, and Geeta Patel. "Area Impossible: Notes toward an Introduction." *GLQ* 22, no. 2 (2016): 151–71.

Das Gupta, Monisha. *Unruly Immigrants: Rights, Activism, and Transnational South Asian Politics in the United States*. Durham: Duke University Press, 2006.

Dharmoo, Gabriel. "Bijuriya Chamke!: Curating My Drag Sound." Post45, 2022, https://post45.org/2022/12/bijuriya-chamke-curating-my-drag-sound/.

Gaind-Krishnan, Sonia. "Qawwali." In *The SAGE International Encyclopedia of Music and Culture*, edited by Janet Sturman, 1776–77. Thousand Oaks, CA: SAGE Publications, Inc., 2019.

Gaind-Krishnan, Sonia. "Qawwali Routes: Notes on a Sufi Music's Transformation in Diaspora." *Religions* 11, no. 12 (2020): 685 (1–16).

Gopinath, Gayatri. *Impossible Desires: Queer Diasporas and South Asian Public Cultures*. Durham: Duke University Press, 2005.

Gorlinsky, Virginia. "Qawwali." Britannica Academic, *Encyclopædia Britannica*, 5 Jun. 2018. academic-eb-com.ezproxy.library.tufts.edu/levels/collegiate/article/qawwali/477174.

Hankins, Sarah. "'I'm a Cross between a Clown, a Stripper, and a Streetwalker': Drag Tipping, Sex Work, and a Queer Sociosexual Economy." *Signs: Journal of Women in Culture and Society* 40, no. 2 (2015): 441–66.

Jabbar, Talib. "Drag Queens in Stars and Stripes." Post45, 2022, accessed September 14, 2024, https://post45.org/2022/12/drag-queens-in-stars-and-stripes/.

Johnson, E. Patrick. "Feeling the Spirit in the Dark: Expanding Notions of the Sacred in the African-American Gay Community." *Callaloo* 21, no. 2 (1998): 399–416.

Kasmani, Omar. *Pakistan Desires: Queer Futures Elsewhere*. Durham: Duke University Press, 2023.

Kasmani, Omar. *Queer Companions: Religion, Public Intimacy, and Saintly Affects in Pakistan*. Durham: Duke University Press, 2022.

Khubchandani, Kareem. "The Land of Disco: Arshia Haq's Insurgent Curation at Discostan." In *Disco!: Music, Image, Dance*, edited by Mimi Haddon, Michael Lawrence, and Arabella Stanger. Oxford: Oxford University Press, forthcoming 2025.

Khubchandani, Kareem. "Terrifying Performances: Black–Brown–Queer Borrowings in *Loins of Punjab Presents*." *Journal of Asian American Studies* 19, no. 3 (2016): 275–97.

Kun, Josh D. "The Aural Border." *Theatre Journal* 52, no. 1 (2000): 1–21.

Mahmood, Rafay, and Richard David Williams. "A Soundtrack for Reimagining Pakistan? Coke Studio, Memory and the Music Video." *Bioscope: South Asian Screen Studies* 10, no. 2 (2020): 111–28.

Paik, A. Naomi. *Bans, Walls, Raids, Sanctuary: Understanding U.S. Immigration for the Twenty-First Century*. Berkeley, CA: University of California Press, 2020.

Pollock, Della. "The Performative 'I.'" *Cultural Studies, Critical Methodologies* 7, no. 3 (2007): 239–55.

Power-Sotomayor, Jade. "Moving Borders and Dancing in Place: Son Jarocho's Speaking Bodies at the Fandango Fronterizo." *TDR: The Drama Review* 64, no. 4 (2020): 84–107.

Qureshi, Abdullah. "Mythologial Migrations." https://mythologicalmigrations.com/about/.

Qureshi, Regula. *Sufi Music of India and Pakistan: Sound, Context and Meaning in Qawwali*. Oxford: Oxford University Press, 2006.

Rahaim, Matthew. *Musicking Bodies: Gesture and Voice in Hindustani Music*. Middletown, CT: Wesleyan University Press, 2012.

Rana, Junaid Akram. *Terrifying Muslims: Race and Labor in the South Asian Diaspora*. Durham: Duke University Press, 2011.

Sangari, Dhruv. "The Story Behind 'Damadam Mast Qalandar.'" 2019, www.musicplus.in/story-behind-damadam-mast-qalandar/.

Shah, Nayan. "Sexuality, Identity, and the Uses of History." In *Q & A:*

Queer in Asian America, edited by David L. Eng and Alice Y. Hom. Philadelphia: Temple University Press, 1998.

Shroff, Sara. "Between Mother and Daughter: Brown Erotics and Sacred Notes." *Journal of Lesbian Studies* 26, no. 1 (2021): 45–52.

Shroff, Sara. "Bold Women, Bad Assets: Honour, Property and Techno-Promiscuities." *Feminist Review* 128, no. 1 (2021): 62–78.

Shroff, Sara. "Fashioning Sufi: Body Politics of Androgynous Sacred Aesthetics." *Feminist Theory* 23, no. 3 (2022): 407–19.

Yusuf, Suhail, and Muhammad Umar. "Dama Dam Mast Qalandar: The Man Behind the Melody." 2014, www.dawn.com/news/1100498.

CONCLUSION How to Grieve

Adeyemi, Kemi. *Feels Right: Black Queer Women and the Politics of Partying in Chicago*. Durham: Duke University Press, 2022.

Buckland, Fiona. "Mr. Mesa's Ticket: Memory and Dance at the Body Positive T-Dance." In *Impossible Dance: Club Culture and Queer World-Making*. Middletown, CT: Wesleyan University Press, 2002.

Chambers-Letson, Joshua Takano. *After the Party: A Manifesto for Queer of Color Life*. New York: New York University Press, 2018.

Chambers-Letson, Joshua. *Queer Love and Loss*. New York: NYU Press, forthcoming.

Cvetkovich, Ann. *An Archive of Feelings: Trauma, Sexuality, and Lesbian Public Cultures*. Durham: Duke University Press, 2003.

Errázuriz, Tomás, and Emilia Müller. "'My Cherished Garment': Rethinking Fashion, Attachment and Durability." *Fashion Theory* 27, no. 3 (2023): 327–54.

Freeman, Elizabeth. *Time Binds: Queer Temporalities, Queer Histories*. Durham: Duke University Press, 2010.

Hanhardt, Christina B. *Safe Space: Gay Neighborhood History and the Politics of Violence*. Durham: Duke University Press, 2013.

Kheshti, Roshanak. "Pocodisco: The Sonic Performativity of

Grief, Grievance, and Joy in Diaspora." *American Anthropologist* (2023).

Kwan, SanSan. *Love Dances: Loss and Mourning in Intercultural Collaboration*. Oxford: Oxford University Press, 2021.

Mattson, Greggor. *Who Needs Gay Bars?: Bar-Hopping through America's Endangered LGBTQ+ Places*. Stanford: Redwood Press, 2023.

Muñoz, José Esteban. "Feeling Brown: Ethnicity and Affect in Ricardo Bracho's 'The Sweetest Hangover (and Other STDs).'" *Theatre Journal* 52, no. 1 (2000): 67–79.

Patel, Shailja. *Migritude*. New York: Kaya Press, 2010.

Pierce, Joseph M. "Our Queer Breath." *QED* 3, no. 3 (2016): 132–34.

Reddy, Vanita. "Femme Migritude: Shailja Patel's Afro-Asian Poetics." *The Minnesota Review*, no. 94 (2020): 67.

Rivera-Servera, Ramón H. "History in Drag: Latina/o Queer Affective Circuits in Chicago." In *Latina/o Midwest Reader*, edited by Omar Valerio-Jiménez, Santiago R. Vaquera-Vásquez, and Claire F. Fox, 185–96. Champaign: University of Illinois Press, 2017.

Román, David. *Acts of Intervention: Performance, Gay Culture, and AIDS*. Bloomington: Indiana University Press, 1998.

Román, David. "Dance Liberation." *Theatre Journal* 55, no. 3 (2003): vii–xxiv.

Sedgwick, Eve Kosofsky. *Touching Feeling: Affect, Pedagogy, Performativity*. Durham: Duke University Press, 2003.

Sharpe, Christina Elizabeth. *In the Wake: On Blackness and Being*. Durham: Duke University Press, 2016.

Shroff, Sara. "Between Mother and Daughter: Brown Erotics and Sacred Notes." *Journal of Lesbian Studies* 26, no. 1 (2021): 45–52.

Torres, Justin. "In Praise of Latin Night at the Queer Club." In *Queer Dance*, edited by Clare Croft. New York: Oxford University Press, 2017.

Tyburczy, Jennifer. "Orlando and the Militancy of Queer Mourning." *QED* 3, no. 3 (2016): 142–46.

Vuong, Ocean. *On Earth We're Briefly Gorgeous: A Novel*. New York: Penguin Press, 2019.

LIST OF ILLUSTRATIONS

COVER AND TITLE SPREAD

Aunty is painted for the gawds, ready to perform at Shia Ho's annual *Made in Asia*, a night of pan-Asian drag at 3 Dollar Bill in Brooklyn. She spent several nights rhinestoning her sari, a yellow and green ombré polyester look she bought on Bangalore's Commercial Street. With the sari she carries a blue leather purse designed by Bahujan-led fashion house Chamar. Her pink bindi is a little off center, just like her. A bit of low fashion, a bit of high fashion, and something askew. A quintessential aunty ensemble. Photos by Davide Laffe. Brooklyn, New York. Used with permission.

INTRODUCTION Lessons in Drag

The host of *Dragistan 2024* at 3 Dollar Bill in Brooklyn. This night brought together twenty South Asian drag artists performing across language, nation, diaspora, and genre. LaWhore is posing in the bar's fuchsia bathroom, wearing a beaded blouse by Calcutta-based designer Dev R Nil, as well as her mother's necklace and her mother's wedding reception sari—a chocolate-brown chiffon with geometric patterns of hand-sewn gold sequins. Sparkle aunty, sparkle! Photo by Mettie Ostrowski, 2024. Brooklyn, New York. Used with permission.

CHAPTER ONE How to Do Research

Just a little close reading! Performing her show *Lessons in Drag* at Brandeis University in 2022, LaWhore sports a pair of yellow spectacles to complement her jumpsuit as she performs a number about the Indian winning streak at the US National Spelling Bee. LaWhore translates Kareem's research on model minority performance through the eager Indian child, committed to being better at the English language than their white counterparts. She is serving "aunty neutrals" in matching snakeskin belt and boots paired with leopard-print jumpsuit and gloves. Photo by Tim Correira, 2022. Waltham, Massachusetts. Used with permission.

CHAPTER TWO How to Be a Drag Queen

Oh, the drama! As she removes her fur coat to reveal a fully beaded gown, LaWhore belts out (lip-synchs) Whitney Houston's "I Will Always Love You." She is debuting her newest show *Aunty Social* at a weekend-long symposium celebrating the intellectual and artistic legacy of D. Soyini Madison. This photo was taken at Northwestern University, Kareem's PhD alma mater. Coincidentally, LaWhore is performing here in the *very* theatre in which she debuted in 2009 with the show *Material Boy*. Photo by Justin Barbin, 2024. Evanston, Illinois. Used with permission.

CHAPTER THREE How to Teach

Sharing the stage with a cast of her students, Professor Vagistan opens the showcase of solo acts that her 2022 "Critical Drag" class prepared in Tufts University's Balch Arena. You see LaWhore in the throes of performing "Rather Be" by Jess Glynne and Clean Bandit, rigorously color-coordinated in the colors of the pansexual flag—she only learned this was the pan flag well after the show! In addition to the student performances, the night featured a cabaret-style set designed by student Kiera O'Connor, and LaWhore's neon gown was constructed and designed by student Claire Ammirato (with the mentorship of Meghan Pearson). The wig was styled by Kareem's colleague Akeem Celestine and the soft-pink lighting was thanks to Brian Lilienthal. It takes a whole department, students and faculty, to look this good. Photo by nik lee, 2022. Medford, Massachusetts. Used with permission.

CHAPTER FOUR How to Be an Aunty

Draped on the stairs of Paragon Nightclub in Brooklyn's Bushwick, LaWhore recovers from a night of emceeing, performing, and several quick changes at the celebration of musician Ali Sethi's fortieth birthday. Her heavy blush, highly arched eyebrows, and blonde hair make her look more aunty than ever. The most aunty thing about this image is that she forced her own drag child, RuAfza, to take this boudoir-style photo. Scandalizing the youth one sultry photo at a time. Notice her drooping rose, her watermelon blouse in solidarity with Gaza, and her very sheer black chiffon sari with gold and black beadwork. A vision! Photo by RuAfza, 2024. Brooklyn, New York. Used with permission.

CHAPTER FIVE How to Write

The library is open! Literally! Tisch Library at Tufts University stayed open extra late on Friday April 20, 2018, for the final showcase of LaWhore's first-ever "Critical Drag" class. The library, the beating heart of the university campus, felt like the most appropriate place to host this night. Because reading is what? Fundamental! This glamour shot shows off LaWhore in a green "sequence gown" with faux fur stole, long black gloves, and dirty blonde straight hair. Photo by Tim Correira, 2018. Medford, Massachusetts. Used with permission.

CHAPTER SIX How to Be a Map

Alight in shine, she spins to become a disco ball. LaWhore layers a gold sequin coat on a copper and turquoise anarkali, over mint and gold sharara pants. And as she turns, they flare outward, each catching the wind and the light. She burns the image with her fire-red hair in this qawwali number, performed for rage, hope, grief, and beauty. This centrifugal stunner was photographed during LaWhore's 2022 visit to Brandeis University. Photo by Tim Correira, 2022. Waltham, Massachusetts. Used with permission.

CONCLUSION How to Grieve

Despite all the color, texture, and pattern, this is a somber moment. LaWhore's eyes are closed as she disappears inward. She lip-synchs to Atif Aslam's soulful voice at the Rose Kennedy Greenway in Boston, performing in front of a mural titled "Your Spirit Whispering in My Ear" by Indigenous artist Jeffrey Gibson. Gibson's painting features patterns inspired by Native beadwork techniques and protest pins with slogans on them; it invokes legacies of creativity and resilience that nourish the future. This photograph distills the capacity for drag to hold fabulosity and grief simultaneously. Photo by Steve Osemwenkhae, 2024. Boston, Massachusetts. Used with permission.

ACKNOWLEDGMENTS

And when the party is over, LaWhore just wants to look slutty and have her photo taken! Here she is at Cherry Grove, New York's legendary Ice Palace on Fire Island, posing with artist extraordinaire Marcel Alcalá. A perfectly vain moment. Thanks for coming to the party! Photo by Koitz, 2023. Fire Island, New York. Used with permission.

ABOUT THE AUTHORS

KAREEM KHUBCHANDANI is the author of two award-winning books, *Decolonize Drag* (2023) and *Ishtyle: Accenting Gay Indian Nightlife* (2020). He is also the co-editor of the Lambda Literary Award finalist *Queer Nightlife* (2021). He serves as associate professor of Theatre, Dance, and Performance Studies at Tufts University.

LAWHORE VAGISTAN is your favorite aunty's favorite aunty—always overdressed, overeducated, and overopinionated. Her music videos, including "Sari" and "There's a Stranger in My House," have been featured at film festivals in Mississauga, Hyderabad, Austin, and San Francisco. In 2009, she co-founded the queer South Asian party *Jai Ho!* in Chicago, and in 2023, she launched *Dragistan*, an annual South Asian drag showcase in New York.